AF809445

Harrison James is a survivor, award-winning activist and co-founder of the acclaimed #YourReferenceAintRelevant campaign. After being sexually abused by his stepmother between the ages of thirteen and sixteen, Harrison has become driven by his personal experiences and is dedicated to reforming Australia's legal system for survivors. For years, he carried the weight of this secret in silence; but now, in his late twenties, his tireless activism has fuelled legislative reform across multiple Australian jurisdictions. He spotlights survivor-led initiatives, showcasing resilience and determination in pursuit of justice and healing. His extraordinary journey has been a beacon of hope for countless individuals, and his unwavering commitment inspires a safer world for all.

Harrison James is a breath of fresh air in the activism space. His determination, his passion, his eloquence and ability to connect with the public and politicians alike is the key to his success. He is a true testament to the importance of activism and spotlighting the victim-survivor experience. This book has the potential to change the political landscape of this country, even if every person who reads it walks away only a little bit more like Harrison James.

Abbie Chatfield

With clear-eyed courage, Harrison gives an insightful meditation on power, justice and what it means to endure. A vital contribution to an urgent conversation.

Brittany Higgins

Harrison has transformed his traumatic experiences into a beacon of hope and change. This book is both a testament to the power of survivor voices and a practical roadmap for anyone ready to turn their story into advocacy. His courage in sharing his journey and his generosity in offering tangible tools for others makes this essential reading. This book doesn't just inspire but equips us all to create the change we need to see.

Chanel Contos, Founder & CEO of Teach Us Consent

Unflinching, practical and full of heart. *Transform Your Pain into Purpose* is the book for anyone who wants to make a difference.

Tarang Chawla

They say you shouldn't gush too much in a book endorsement. It might look inauthentic or paid for. But Harrison didn't reach out to me; I reached out to him. Not as an actor or an activist, but as a survivor with questions. Harrison had broken his silence, and I wanted to know how he had done it. In this incredible book, he will teach you the same. When Harrison writes 'we need a world that doesn't leave people behind', he doesn't just mean it; he lives it. I have read this book twice, and by the time it goes to print, I will have read it again. Thank you, Harrison.

Ruby Rose

Harrison James is one of Australia's most impactful advocates. In sharing his story, Harri empowers others to tell theirs. It is an absolute privilege to know Harri, to witness his work and to now know him at a deeper level through this book. This is what modern masculinity in Australia looks like: courage, vulnerability and action. I am inspired by Harri's strength every single day. This book is a reminder of how each of us has the power to make significant change in the world.

Hannah Ferguson

Harrison James

TRANSFORM YOUR PAIN INTO PURPOSE

How to find your voice and make a difference

affirm press

affirm press

First published in Australia in 2026 by Affirm Press,
a Simon & Schuster (Australia) Pty Limited company
Wurundjeri Woiwurrung Country
Level 3, 162 Collins Street, Melbourne VIC 3000

Affirm Press is located on the unceded land of the Wurundjeri Woiwurrung peoples of the Kulin Nation. Affirm Press pays respect to their Elders past and present.

New York Amsterdam/Antwerp London Toronto Sydney/Melbourne New Delhi
Visit our website at www.simonandschuster.com.au

AFFIRM PRESS and design are trademarks of Affirm Press Pty Ltd, Inc., used under licence by Simon & Schuster, LLC.

10 9 8 7 6 5 4 3 2 1

NATIONAL LIBRARY OF AUSTRALIA

A catalogue record for this book is available from the National Library of Australia

9781923293892 (paperback)
9781761825651 (ebook)

Cover design by Nada Backovic
Interior design and typeset by Post Pre-press Group in Adobe Caslon Pro
Printed and bound in Australia by the Opus Group

FSC www.fsc.org MIX Paper from responsible sources FSC® C001695

AUTHOR'S NOTE

This book explores themes that may be difficult or distressing for some readers, including child sexual abuse, domestic and family violence, sexual assault, court experiences, homophobia, misogyny, trauma responses, suicide and mental health issues.

While no further content warnings appear throughout, I encourage you to move through the pages in a way that feels safe for you.

If you are a survivor and feel impacted by anything you read, support is available. Full Stop Australia offers free, 24/7 telephone and online counselling. You can reach them at 1800 FULL STOP (1800 385 578) or visit fullstop.org.au.

Please take care with yourself as you read.

For Bella, Mum, Grandma and Hannah.
The girls who get me through.

CONTENTS

INTRODUCTION

Experiencing sexual abuse as a child is fucked.

I've racked my brain for days trying to find a better word – something more sophisticated, more academic, maybe even profound. Something I could say in a roomful of people without the slight flinch, the subtle silence, and the shift in body language when they act like they know what to say, but it's painfully obvious they don't. Child sexual abuse is 'complex'? Sure. 'Traumatic'? Absolutely. 'Incomprehensible'? That doesn't even begin to cover it.

People want you to say something 'appropriate', something they can nod along to. Something that doesn't make them squirm in their seats or corrupt their shiny, filtered view of life where everything is #amazeballs.

They want 'healing' and 'overcoming' when the reality is far from that. The reality is anger. Confusion. A constant fight just to exist without falling apart. Abuse warps your sense of safety, completely distorts your understanding of love and rewires your brain in ways you'll spend years – if not a lifetime – trying to untangle.

'Fucked' is the only word that truly captures the full

catastrophe of child sexual abuse. It's the only word that feels right; that doesn't try to make it neat or acceptable or tie it in a bow. It just is what it is.

And if that makes you uncomfortable, good. Because, as I'll explore at length in this book, it's only in discomfort that we begin to understand the need for change.

Life has a way of throwing each of us into places we never thought we'd be. I believe we all deserve the tools, support and time to find our way out of those places, whether we are there through our own actions or not, in whatever way we can. Some people do it with therapy, others with protest. Some are still trying. Some can't.

We need a world that doesn't leave people behind.

You may have bought this book because you're a survivor like me, or maybe you've been following my activism for the last few years, or maybe you just saw it in the bargain bin of a major chain store where all good books go to die.

However this book ended up in your hands, I'm glad you're here. I hope you're reading it for the same reason I wrote it: to make a genuine difference. Whether you're hoping to change the whole world, your community or simply your own home, whatever you have capacity for, I've filled these pages with ideas and inspiration to help you begin.

You don't have to have experienced the devastation of child sexual abuse. Maybe you've survived cancer or a natural disaster or war. Maybe you've lost your grandmother, or you're going through a break-up, or maybe you're pissed off because hospital parking costs $70 a day and you've been in and out of appointments for months. Whatever you've had to overcome, big or small, this book is for you.

Because here's the thing: we all have far more influence than we ever give ourselves credit for. It doesn't matter whether your pain was life-altering or something that feels less dramatic in comparison – it's still real, it's still yours and it still matters. This book is about taking that pain, no matter what it looks like, and acquiring the tools to turn it into something that creates legitimate, lasting change. Some of us come out of pain ready to fight for everyone who's ever been hurt like we have, and some of us are searching for a way to save ourselves – both are powerful, and both are important.

But before we dive into that, I'm going to tell you my story.

I am a survivor of child sexual abuse. That chapter of my life was dark and messy, and shattered me in ways I didn't think I'd ever come back from. But I did. I found the pieces, and I put them back together. Not perfectly; not the way they were before. Because the truth is, the person I am now isn't the person I would've been if the abuse never happened. And I think that's something people don't always understand: that when you survive something like this, you don't just 'go back' to who you were. That version of you is gone. What's left is someone new. Someone rebuilt. My story is one of survival, yes, but it's also about transformation. Because somewhere along the way, I decided the pain that tried to break me wasn't going to be the thing that defined me. Because real transformation isn't just about finding purpose or trying to change the world; sometimes, it's about something much simpler, and much harder. It's about deciding that the cycle of abuse ends with you. That whatever was done to you, whatever pain you've carried, it doesn't get to keep echoing through the people you love. It doesn't get to shape the kind of partner or parent you are, or will be. It doesn't get to control how you handle anger, or what you reach for when you're hurting. That choice to stop the cycle might not look like much from the outside, but if all you ever do with your pain is make sure it ends with you, then you've changed the world in one of the most important ways there is.

Now, don't get me wrong. I didn't wake up one morning with a sudden surge of inspiration and a well-crafted life's purpose. There was no montage of me journalling in a sunlit room or triumphantly climbing a metaphorical mountain. Most days were a hell of a lot messier. In fact, most days were shit. My healing wasn't linear, because it never truly is. But eventually, through a lot of hard work, therapy and more setbacks than I care to count, I found my way through. And, to be honest, I'm still finding it. Healing isn't a task you complete; it's something you live with. Something you keep choosing, over and over again, every day you decide to keep going. Some days you do it gracefully. Other days you just survive.

I'm sharing this with you not because I have all the answers – trust me, I don't – but because I know what it's like to feel like the weight of your experience is too much to carry. I know what it's like to feel angry at the world, to grieve what was taken from you and to wonder if happiness is something you'll ever get to feel again.

I also know what it's like to push beyond that. To find meaning in the thing that nearly destroyed you, and to eventually reach a point where, after fighting so hard for change, you realise you're allowed to stop and rest. You're allowed to want more than survival, or purpose or even justice. You're allowed to want a life that feels like yours.

So, I'm honoured to share my story with you. Not because it's polished or perfect, but because it's real. My hope is that, somewhere in these pages, you'll find something that resonates – a story that mirrors your own, a tool you can try, or even just a sentence that sticks with you when you need it most. Maybe it'll be the moment you finally write the email you've been avoiding. Maybe it'll be the push to speak up in a space where you've always stayed silent. Or maybe it'll simply be the reminder that, even after everything, you're still here – and that counts for more than you know.

Because if there's one thing I've learned, it's that even the worst parts of our lives can become catalysts for something greater than us as individuals.

I was sexually abused by my stepmother every day, before and after school, between the ages of thirteen and sixteen. When I was fifteen, she gave birth to my daughter, a child I wasn't allowed to call my own. For years, I had to pretend my baby was my sister, smiling for family photos, blowing out candles at birthday parties, opening Christmas presents, all while holding onto a secret so heavy it felt like I could drown in it. I sat through dinners where no one knew, went to school like nothing had happened and carried on as if I wasn't suffocating under the weight of it all.

My parents divorced when I was ten. The years leading up to their split were a blur of constant fighting – arguments that were always louder and more intense than any child should ever witness. My father was physically, verbally and emotionally abusive – a man who would come home in drunken rampages, pin me down by the neck with the full weight of his body, call me a 'poof' for dancing and catapult cutlery at my four-year-old skull. The fear I felt of my father was woven into the air I breathed, the sound of his keys in the door, the unpredictability of how each night would end. I spent those years feeling unseen, as if I were just a spectator to the chaos, trapped in the dysfunctional crossfire of my parents' hatred for each other. In separate conversations, they would mention things about each other – sometimes out of anger, sometimes out of pain and sometimes, I think, just because they didn't know who else to turn to – but as a child, I didn't have the emotional tools to hold those things. I didn't understand that adults could be complicated, contradictory or even cruel. So I did what kids do: I internalised everything. My emotions swung between loving my mother and resenting my father, to resenting my mother and siding with my father. Back and forth, again and again, until I didn't know who or what I believed. All I knew was that the ground beneath me never felt steady.

Eventually, after nearly three years without seeing my dad, I decided to move in with him. Not because he had changed – he hadn't – but because I was a boy just starting high school and desperate for a father figure, even one who always made me feel like I was walking on eggshells, never knowing when he'd explode. As warped as it sounds now, his version of masculinity – volatile, aggressive, domineering – was all I knew. It was what I thought being a 'man' was. That was my baseline. Because I needed something – someone – and at the time, I thought that someone had to be him.

After moving in, my stepmother came into my life. She offered something I didn't even realise I was missing: attention, care and the feeling that, for once, I wasn't invisible. At least, that's what it looked like. That's what it was *meant* to look like.

What she was really doing was setting the stage – making me feel seen so she could make sure I stayed focused on her. What felt like comfort was actually control; what was crafted to feel like care was the beginning of grooming.

What I craved more than anything was warmth, safety and someone to show me that I mattered and, for a while, I thought she was that person. She made me feel seen. She made me feel heard. And yes, for the first time, I felt like I was loved.

My biological mum has always loved me more than anything – I know that now – but at the time, she was a single mother raising four children, trying to hold our world together after a decade of violence. She was doing her absolute best: surviving, shielding us, carrying more than any one person should have to. At thirteen, when I moved in with my father, I didn't realise how much Mum was holding. Caught in the emotional wreckage of it all, I thought I had to pick a side of my parents' divorce, so I chose my dad – not because Mum failed me, but because I didn't understand what love could look like when someone was just trying to stay afloat.

In that, my stepmother saw an opening.

It first began one night at Hoyts Cinema in Sydney's Entertainment Quarter. We were there to watch *Step Up 4: Miami Heat* (otherwise known as *Step Up: Revolution* – honestly, I don't understand why the producers at Universal Studios needed two titles). During the film, my stepmother softly ran her fingers along my legs. It was a discreet action that took me by surprise, but as a thirteen-year-old boy going through puberty, I found it surprisingly pleasant to be touched by an older woman. After all, it was the kind of 'ultimate fantasy' I often saw in internet porn – I was on cloud nine! She held my hand, kissed me on the cheek and, when the movie ended, we caught the bus home, cuddling one another. I remember the walk up the hill from the bus stop, arms wrapped around each other in a way that felt odd and sneaky but somehow not wrong. Then she asked, 'Are you like this with your real mum?'

I didn't know how to answer, and I froze. And then, without thinking, I said, 'Oh no, never.'

Can you see what she was doing? From the very start, she was making me feel complicit – like it was something we were both choosing, both responsible for. And it worked.

What I didn't understand back then was how easily you can become dependent on a feeling someone gives you, especially when you've been starved of it. It's not love, but it feels like it. It's not safety, but it's safer than being unnoticed. That kind of attention is addictive in its own way, and once you've felt it, you'll do almost anything not to lose it.

The next few days blurred together. The touching became more frequent, more intimate, more explicit. She'd ride the bus with me to school, and we'd make sure to sit in the back row, where no one could see us. We'd hold hands. We'd kiss. It felt wrong, but it also felt like it was our secret. I didn't have the words to explain it, and I couldn't tell anyone.

By the following Wednesday, it had escalated further. My father was away in Queensland for business – he went every Wednesday, back when his company was just starting up. It was then that the first penetrative act of sexual abuse was committed.

It continued when my father wasn't around and it was just me and my stepmother. He was gone early in the mornings and returned late in the evenings, so I endured the sexual abuse every day, both before and after school. What I couldn't comprehend was that what my stepmother was doing wasn't affection, it wasn't a clandestine 'affair', or anything else I might have thought it was. It was deception. It was exploitation. It was torture. It was abuse disguised as 'love'.

I wish I could say I saw it for what it was right away. But the truth is, I didn't. I was just a thirteen-year-old kid. The lines were blurred, and the manipulation was so subtle, so incremental, that by the time I realised how wrong it was, I was already drowning in it.

Once you're in that deep, the shame keeps you in that terrible cycle. I told myself I'd ruin my family. I told myself no one would believe me.

I thought I was in love with my stepmother, and the constant coercion and grooming made me feel complicit in the abuse, ultimately leading me to stay silent for years. She told me I was special, mature for my age. She said she understood me in a way no one else did. And when you're a kid starving for attention, desperate to feel wanted, you cling to that – even when it's completely twisted.

She didn't just make me feel special, she made herself feel like the only safe place. Like she was the only one who really understood what was happening, the only person I could relax around, the only one who knew the truth. Everyone else became a threat to her, and to the 'secret'. In a world that often equates vulnerability with weakness, I carried the weight of silence, believing it was my duty to protect my stepmother.

My stepmother told me I was 'the man in this relationship'. She made me believe it was my responsibility to provide for her, to protect her and to love her the way an adult man loves a woman. She groomed me. She would touch me. She stole my virginity. She sexually abused me in my bed, in the shower, in the living room and in the kitchen. There was nowhere she didn't have absolute control over me. She made me believe we were in a forbidden relationship that my father could never know about. That this was something secret, something special. She told me it was love. She would take me on 'dates' to Italian restaurants. She made me believe I wanted it and persuaded me to think it was normal.

My stepmother convinced me that if anyone ever found out, 'we would both go to jail'. She said both, as if I had any power in this situation. As if I was anything other than her victim. And so, every time I saw a police car driving on the street, my stomach would drop. I'd panic, convinced this was it. That I was about to be arrested, exposed, ruined and revealed as the teen who 'fucked' his dad's wife. That the whole world would see me the way she made me see myself – like I was guilty. The fear she cemented in me kept me silent and compliant. She made damn sure I would never speak a word of it to anyone. And, for years, I didn't.

She would watch me sleep, standing over me like it was normal; like it was a sweet gesture or something affectionate. But it was calculated and controlled. She was monitoring whether or not I was still complicit in protecting her. I see that now. I see how it was never about affection but about surveillance. About making sure I was still under her thumb. About making sure I hadn't woken up, hadn't cracked, hadn't started thinking for myself. It was about her fear and anxiety over the fact that I might let something slip, that the carefully built lie she had constructed might crumble if I dared to speak. So she studied every facet of my existence to make sure that her secret – which was that she was sexually abusing a child – was still safe. And I hate that I let her.

My stepmother constructed this scenario and ensured that everything I did, every move I made, was in service of protecting her secret. She manipulated me so deeply that I didn't even realise I was being manipulated. That's the thing about control: when it's done slowly and gradually enough, it starts to feel like your own idea. I thought I was just being mature. Responsible. Protecting the woman I loved. I thought I was choosing this. But the truth is, she regularly chipped away at my sense of self until I didn't know where she ended and I began.

Before I go any further, I need to paint a picture of my father so you can understand the entirety of the situation and the atmosphere of fear that I grew up in.

People often ask me about him. Did he know? Did he see anything? Did he ever step in? Did he care? How could he not have noticed?

Well, I think so. Yes. No. I don't believe he did. And I wish I knew.

My father is not a father, he's a sperm donor. Long before my stepmother ever entered the picture, he made me believe I was worthless before I even had the chance to figure out who I was. His presence turned the house into a minefield: quiet on the surface but a constant angst that today might be the day that everything blows up. I lived in fear of his voice, his footsteps down the hallway, the sound of the front door slamming. I was utterly terrified of him. And it wasn't fear like a jump scare in a horror film, it was fear like a background noise. I mean the kind of fear that lives in your bones and shapes your every thought. The kind of fear that makes your stomach drop at the sound of keys in the door. The kind of fear that makes you rehearse conversations in your head before you speak, just to avoid saying something that may set him off. It was the kind of fear that convinces you you're in danger, even when no one's there, because your body doesn't know the difference anymore.

Dad would call me a 'fairy'. A 'cat'. He mocked the way I spoke, the way I walked, the clothes I wore. He hated the fact that I did drama lessons. That I loved art. He hated that when I was ten, I danced like Michael Jackson. I wore all the bedazzled costumes, set up a speaker on the front deck and invited the whole street to come watch me perform, all to raise money for the Sydney Children's Hospital. I was just a ten-year-old kid trying to bring a little joy into the world, and he made me feel like I was a total embarrassment. I was too soft. I was too much. He made me ashamed of the things that made me *me*. He taught me that masculinity meant cruelty; that love was conditional, and something I had to earn by being less of myself.

He choked me more times than I care to remember, including once in front of my then best mate. He would come home in drunken rampages, and his violence was like a cyclone tearing through the house. I remember one night when he stormed into my room, his face as red as the rage he carried, cornering Mum with his belt pulled off and ready to strike. I was eight years old, on the top bunk, frozen, crying, watching it all unfold. And then I jumped. I launched myself onto his back because, even at eight, I knew if I didn't do something, he was going to hurt my mother.

I never felt like I was enough in his eyes. No matter what I did, no matter how hard I tried, he always found something to tear me down with. And somehow, when he caught my stepmother kissing me in my bed when I was fourteen years old, he decided to blame me. He saw what was happening with his own fucking eyes, and instead of protecting me, instead of holding her accountable, instead of finally stepping up and being the father I so desperately needed, he decided it was my fault. He looked at his son being sexually abused, and he made the choice to see an accomplice instead of a victim. The next morning, I woke up to an empty house. I remember getting myself ready for school, tying my cerise and blue Marcellin College tie, when the phone rang. It was him. He went ballistic on me; called me an 'embarrassment' and said, 'If I ever catch you doing that again, you watch what I fucking do to you.' Then I put my backpack on and went to school with tears rolling down my cheeks. I was in Year 8.

And, to this day, he still flies to the Philippines to see my stepmother. As if nothing ever happened. As if she didn't tear my life apart. That is a fucking choice. It's a blatant slap in the face to everything I've been through. A constant, deliberate reminder that he chooses her. He hasn't just dismissed what happened; he's minimised it, mocked it and done everything in his power to twist the truth I've spoken, all to protect his own image and ego. Because deep down, he cannot stand the fact that I've called him out for exactly what he is: an abusive, cowardly, manipulative, gaslighting, tyrannical, sociopathic, narcissistic, insecure little cunt who is terrified of being exposed and hopes that eventually I'll just shut up and go away.

When I was fifteen, when the daily instances of sexual abuse had been going on for two years, I was staying with my mum for a couple of weeks while my dad and stepmother were on holiday in Thailand. I was sitting on the 360 bus from Bondi Junction to Clovelly Beach, still in my school uniform, passing the Waverley Bowling Club with only a few stops to go before I was home.

My phone buzzed with a message from my stepmother on Facebook Messenger. I wasn't expecting much, probably just checking in or saying something small. Instead, she told me she was pregnant.

I felt my stomach drop. Everything in me tightened as I stared at the screen. I couldn't think. Couldn't breathe. The bus was packed with other schoolkids – laughing, talking, fighting over seats – and I was sitting there, trying to process the f§act that I might be about to become a father. I remember thinking, *This is it. We're going to jail. Dad is going to find out. He's going to kill me. Everyone will know.* It felt like the world was caving in on me and there was no way out.

I messaged back: *Don't tell Dad.*

She replied that she already had – and that she'd told him the baby was his.

At the time, I didn't question it. I was too scared, too overwhelmed and, if I'm honest, too relieved that he seemed to believe it. He'd had a vasectomy years earlier, when he was still with my mum, and he'd always said he never went back for the results. I'll never know for certain what my father did or didn't truly know, but I think that, looking back, he wasn't able to face the truth, even to himself – because that would have meant accepting what he had seen and what it meant.

My daughter was born in December 2015. Not long after that, the final act of abuse occurred, on my sixteenth birthday – 7 January 2016 – when my stepmother performed oral sex on me in the kitchen.

A couple of months later, I found myself on a flight to the Philippines with my father, my stepmother and our newborn baby, to introduce the baby to my stepmother's family. We stayed in Angeles City, where she grew up, around three hours from Manila. My dad, who I guess was trying to bond with me in his own strange way, took me out drinking and clubbing in the red-light district – places no sixteen-year-old should have been. I'd never touched alcohol before, but on that first night, I drank so much, so quickly that I ended up so out of it that I shat myself in the shower. My stepmother's sisters and their friends also joined us clubbing during that trip. While my stepmother was at home with the baby, I ended up clubbing with them every night for those two weeks away. One of the women – someone I particularly bonded with – was in her mid-twenties. On the second last night, she invited me out again, just the two of us. I didn't think anything of it at first, but she had booked a nearby motel room in advance, and once we were alone in the room after a heavy night of drinking, she sexually assaulted me.

I froze, like I always had. Convinced myself that I was 'lucky'. In my mind, I didn't have the right to say no. By then, I was so accustomed to being used that I didn't even realise it was assault until much later.

When my stepmother found out the next day, she didn't seem shocked or angry on my behalf, or ask if I was okay. Instead, she used that moment to accuse me of 'cheating' on her – as if what had happened was consensual, as if she had some claim over me. That was her excuse to end what she called 'our relationship'.

Looking back, I can see that this wasn't about betrayal;

this was about opportunity. The abuse had served its purpose and she saw a clean exit. We were too close to being caught, too close to the truth. She needed distance, so she found a way to end it while still holding the power, still casting the blame on me.

When we returned to Australia, I didn't go back to my father's house. I moved into my maternal grandmother's apartment in Maroubra Beach. My father turned my old bedroom into the baby's room.

I was still in school, juggling afternoon shifts at the fish and chip shop across from my father and stepmother's place. I would visit my daughter as often as I could after every shift, then return to my grandmother's place. I said nothing to anyone. That routine – school, work, visits, silence – continued for the next three years. When I was nineteen, I finally moved into my own apartment in Clovelly, deliberately choosing one just around the corner from my father's house. It meant I could see my daughter more often, still under the guise of being her older brother. Sometimes she would even stay over. We'd build forts out of pillows, play Nintendo Switch and watch *Hey Duggee* on repeat – her favourite show at the time. Those moments meant everything to me. They were all I had.

I felt that I needed to be alert at all times. As a teenager I avoided house parties, alcohol, drugs – anything that might lower my guard. My stepmother would make me lie to the people I cared for, over and over again, isolating me, slowly and deliberately. All my friends were out drinking in parks, experimenting, growing up, but I couldn't risk it. I was terrified that if I lost control for even a second, the truth might slip out. So I kept my distance, never allowing anyone to get too close. I even lied about sex, saying I lost my virginity to a girl at a house party, just like the rest of the guys in my group. I felt I had to perform a version of masculinity to stay safe and unquestioned. I was living in a state of relentless anxiety, trying to make sense of a reality that made no sense at all.

My father and I spoke sparingly during those years, except for when I started working at his company in 2019. There was a mutual silence between us, a kind of emotional absenteeism that made it easy to stay disconnected. I was envious of my father. Not because I wanted to be him, but because I believed he had taken the life that was supposed to be mine. He got to be the father, to live with the woman I believed I loved. That envy was tangled in grief, confusion and trauma I didn't have the vocabulary for. I fantasised about running away with my stepmother and our daughter, just the three of us. I thought maybe then, in solitude, the anxiety and rage would stop. The lies could stop. I could breathe again. But, of course, that was never real. It was the story I told myself to survive.

It's taken me years to understand that, even then, while I was in the thick of surviving, I was also doing something extraordinary: I was holding on. I was protecting the one thing that mattered most to me in the world: my daughter. I was being the best father I knew how to be, in the only way I could. And that mattered. It still does.

In 2019, three years after the sexual abuse had ended, I was nineteen and, despite everything, I still viewed my abuser as 'my ex' or 'the mother of my child', and as someone I felt I had to protect at all costs. Beyond that, as a loving father, I felt an overwhelming need to guard my daughter and keep herout of harm's way. The fear of destroying everything, of shattering what little stability I thought I had left, kept me silent and complicit.

My daughter was just three years old and I was still maintaining the lie, pretending to everyone that she was my little half-sister, upholding the story that my father was hers, burying the truth about our connection and the past. One afternoon, I picked her up from preschool, like I did so often, and along our walk home, I treated her to her favourite ice-cream. We sat by the beach, watching the waves crash in and out, and we talked about the silliest things, questions only a child's curious brilliance would think to ask: 'Do fish get thirsty?' 'Are birds scared of heights?' 'Can I be a mermaid when I grow up?'

I remember laughing, answering her questions as best as I could, all while trying to savour the normalcy of it, pretending there was nothing wrong, pretending there were no secrets surrounding us; just some time with my gorgeous girl.

When it was time to go, I dropped her off to my stepmother, her little hand in mine as we walked to the door. She hugged me tight, looked up with those big, trusting eyes and said, 'I'll see you tomorrow, Haz.'

I returned to my apartment later that evening, had dinner, did some work and went to bed with a sense of calm my little girl had gifted me so generously – nothing out of the ordinary.

The next day, my father called me. Again, he was away on business in Queensland, and there was something in his voice that unsettled me immediately. He told me my stepmother wasn't answering her phone, and there were some strange transactions going through on his bank card. He asked me to check on her and the baby.

When I hung up, something didn't sit right. A heaviness

crept in. I tried to brush it off, but deep down, I knew something was wrong. I rushed over and, as soon as I stepped inside, the silence was deafening. It wasn't just quiet; it was hollow. An emptiness, like the house itself had been abandoned by life. Everything was gone; the cupboards were bare, wardrobes emptied. My daughter and my stepmother were gone.

It took a few moments for the full weight of it to hit me, but when it did, it hit hard. My chest tightened and the panic began to set in. 'Where the fuck is my child?' I couldn't think straight, couldn't process what was happening. The world felt like it was closing in.

Hours passed and I found out through my father that they had left for the Philippines – my stepmother's homeland – without telling anyone. She had taken my daughter. They were gone.

A day later, in a desperate attempt to redirect my father's attention, my stepmother sent him an email, falsely accusing me of rape. It worked far too well. My father operates like a Spanish fighting bull – all rage, no pause – and that email was a deliberately dangled red rag. He charged. My dad quickly forwarded the message to both my biological mother and me and, within moments, before I could even finish reading it, I was bombarded with an abusive phone call, demanding an explanation. His voice was venomous and violent. I was in shock, unable to comprehend the few sentences I had read, let alone defend myself.

Then my phone rang again. It was Mum.

She knew something was deeply wrong because she didn't hesitate: 'I'm coming to get you.' Then she hung up.

I didn't even have the strength to get off the floor. I lay

there, crying on the cold grey carpet of my apartment, which was damp with my sweat and tears. Everything was spinning. My lungs felt like they were collapsing in on themselves.

When I saw her car pull up out front, I wiped my face, pulled myself off the floor and ran out the door. I needed to hold it together. I needed to act like I was okay, even though I wasn't. I opened the passenger door and climbed in.

She looked at me, her face tense, scared.

'What happened?' she asked gently.

I stared straight ahead. 'I was in a relationship with [stepmother's name],' I said. 'And there's a good chance [daughter's name] is mine.'

She didn't speak as her face drained of all colour. Her hands stayed locked on the steering wheel. Her eyes were wide. She didn't cry. She didn't ask questions. She just drove. The car felt like it had shrunk around us, as if the weight of the truth had taken up all the space inside. But even in her silence, she didn't leave me alone with it.

When we got back to her house, she gave me the front room to myself. She sat with me on the couch, calm but serious. 'We'll work out what to do next. I'll handle your father. You don't need to talk to him.' We made a plan. I knew she was standing in my corner. She said the words I had been craving to hear since I was a thirteen-year-old boy: 'You're not alone.'

Still, I could see it in her face: the guilt. The heartache. She kept looking at me like I was the same little boy she used to watch draw for hours at the kitchen table, and she couldn't understand how this had happened without her knowing. Like she'd failed me.

The truth is, Mum was manipulated just like I had been.

My stepmother didn't just isolate me – she convinced everyone around me she was a loving, trustworthy woman. She knew how to charm, how to lie, how to build a perfect mask. She made herself look like a safe person, and we all believed her. We were all caught in the web.

But once Mum knew, she acted. She didn't flinch. She didn't deny it. She didn't ask for more proof.

She protected me – the way a parent is supposed to.

When I told Mum, I used the word 'relationship' not because I was in any sort of healthy, consensual bond but because, even after all that time, I still didn't fully understand what had happened. I didn't realise that I had been trapped in an abusive situation. I was nineteen, processing years of trauma, and I hadn't yet grasped that what I thought had been an 'affair' behind my dad's back was actually skilfully performed manipulation and exploitation.

The reality of it didn't sink in until much later. The truth was too overwhelming for me to see clearly. But once I could, the realisation broke me. I was consumed by an overwhelming sense of guilt and shame, and thoughts of self-loathing.

Why didn't I say something earlier?

Why didn't I fight hard enough to keep my daughter here?

I'm not a man, I'm a bitch. I'm a fucking failure.

I hate my fucking father. Look what the prick has driven me to become.

My dad was right, I am a faggot. I'm a pussy.

I have nothing left. I'll just kill myself.

I had lost my daughter, been falsely accused of rape and was only just beginning to understand that my entire childhood had been stolen from me by a paedophile. That realisation didn't arrive all at once – it came in pieces. It came in the horror on other people's faces, in the silence that followed my words. I told a seasoned therapist, one of the best in Sydney, about my story and even his face dropped. That reaction alone confirmed what I was still struggling to accept.

I couldn't handle the mental toll it was taking on me. The weight of everything I had endured made me feel like there was no way out. I didn't want to be here anymore. One Friday afternoon, I was done. I had a plan – one that felt like the only way out. I had mapped it all out in my traumatised mind: I'd crash my car into a sunflower field I remembered on the drive from Sydney to Canberra, somewhere along the Federal Highway, the following Monday morning. I thought that would be it – the end of everything. But before I followed through with my plan, I figured I'd go out with a bang. I decided to drink, take any drug I could get my hands on, sleep with anyone I could get back to my place, and just live out what I thought would be my final weekend.

Saturday night came and I went to a friend's birthday. I went hard. I walked into Dan Murphy's and bought a 700mL bottle of Hennessy Very Special Cognac (twenty-two standard drinks), and a six-pack of cherry-flavoured Coca-Cola, because that was what all my favourite rappers drank, and I wanted to be like them. I mixed it together and drank it all in less than two hours. It didn't take long for the alcohol to take hold. The rest of the night was a total blur. I don't remember much of it, but I've seen the pictures my friends at the time thought would be funny to take of me vomiting on the footpath and lying on a broken beach chair someone had left for the council to collect. I remember two mates dragging me back to my bed and, in my drunken stupor, I took my sleeping meds and antidepressants together, hoping to numb myself further. That night, I dreamt of my mother finding me dead on the floor of my bedroom, and the weight of it crushed me. The next morning, it hit me: I had to change something, or be lost forever.

By Sunday night, I was packing a bag for the Sydney Clinic, an inpatient mental health clinic in Bronte. I didn't know what to expect, but I knew I needed help. I couldn't keep living like this, with everything weighing down on me. I was barely holding on, and I couldn't keep pretending I had it all together. Thankfully, my mother had recently upgraded her private health insurance, which allowed me to get into the rehab centre. It was one of the few times in my life that something felt like it might just save me.

I didn't know how to process the emotions, the memories or the overwhelming truth of everything that had happened to me. I didn't know where to begin, or if I could even fix myself. But I had to try.

It wasn't easy – nothing about it was – but in that moment, I had finally made the decision to live. For once, even in that small sliver of realisation, I wasn't giving up on myself. It wasn't much, but it was enough to push me to seek help. I knew I couldn't keep going down the same path. I remember reading articles about men in their fifties or even sixties who were only just sharing their stories of sexual abuse after decades of silence. I was twenty at the time, and I couldn't bear the thought of carrying this with me for the rest of my life. It struck me that if I didn't confront this, it would follow me into every part of my future, affecting my relationships, my ability to trust, even the way I might raise my future children. I don't know where that foresight came from, but it hit me hard, and it's something that's stayed with me ever since. It was the first time in a long time I had hope, even if it was just a flicker.

I now realise it wasn't my fault that I got to that point. I was dealt a rough fucking hand, but only I had the power and the responsibility to change it. Even if I didn't fully understand how to navigate it all at the time, going to rehab was the best decision I ever made.

That was seven years ago. Even after everything, the pain of losing my daughter still feels as fresh and unbearable as it did that day. My stepmother still lives in the Philippines, in exile, with my daughter.

Losing my daughter, my beautiful little girl, was the most devastating consequence of everything I went through. I would endure my experience 1000 times over if it meant never having to lose my baby. The emptiness of not having her here, not seeing her smile, not hearing her voice, has been a constant ache that never goes away. I've missed every milestone that any parent dreams of being part of. Birthdays and Christmases have come and gone, and I've watched others celebrate those moments with their children, all the while knowing I couldn't. I missed her first day of big school, the excitement of her first loose tooth, and the pure pride that would've lit up her face the moment she realised she could read all by herself. Those tiny, fleeting, precious moments that make parenthood something so incredibly special – the moments when a little girl should have her dad right there. All of that is gone. Those memories I'll never get to make with her, moments I can never get back.

If I had known that the hug she gave me that day would be

the last time I'd hold her, I would never have let go. I would have held her tighter, longer, trying to freeze that moment in time, trying to somehow preserve it, to keep her safe in my arms.

Now, all I have is the silence of her absence. The emptiness in my heart is a constant reminder of what was stolen not just from me, but from her too. A child deserves the love and protection of their parents, and it completely breaks me to know that, right now, I can't be there for her when she needs me most.

There's a cruel irony in the fact that for so many years, I spent all my energy protecting my stepmother. I believed that by keeping her secret, by staying silent, I was doing the right thing. I was conditioned by years of abuse and silence to think that I was complicit in all of it – that somehow, I was a willing participant. The truth is that I was just a vulnerable kid with no voice and no agency, carrying a burden far heavier than anything a child should have to bear. And it wasn't just me who needed protection. It was my daughter too, both of us trapped in this twisted world that was carefully hidden behind closed doors, where the abuse was made invisible and the people who could have helped us remained oblivious.

It's hard to look back and not feel that deep sting of abandonment, not just from my stepmother, but from every adult who was close enough to notice that something wasn't right. I don't know if they truly didn't see it, or if they chose not to. Either way, no one stepped in, even when the signs were there. I wasn't rebellious or loud. I was quiet; too quiet. Hyper-independent, emotionally detached, constantly trying to prove I had it all together. I filled my days with work, routine and responsibility not because I was ambitious, but because staying busy helped keep the chaos at bay. There was no room for rest, no room to feel.

I had a watchfulness that didn't match my age; guarded, cautious with people and found it difficult to trust anyone fully. Even my body language spoke volumes – I flinched at certain types of touch, avoided eye contact when things got too personal and often seemed emotionally absent, like I wasn't fully in the room. No one ever asked why.

The long-term signs of child sexual abuse don't always look like what people expect. They can show up, even years later, in the forms of hypervigilance, chronic anxiety, dissociation, numbing or an exaggerated need to stay in control. Often, the most 'put-together' young person in the room is the one silently holding the heaviest story. That was me. And still, no one saw it.

All these years later, I often wonder how many moments passed where someone could have stepped in. How many adults might have paused and gently asked the right question, or simply stayed close enough to notice the truth. You don't need to know the full story to notice when something's off; you just need to pay attention, and care enough to act.

My daughter, still a preschooler when she was taken, had no voice. She had no way of knowing the truth of what had happened. Worse yet, she had no one to actually protect her. She was ripped away from me and taken to a country where, after years of searching for loopholes in international law, dealing with police involvement and enduring legal trial and error, I still cannot reach her. I think of my daughter every minute of every day, wondering if she remembers those small moments we shared, or if they're lost to her now. I can only imagine the confusion she must have felt, suddenly without her father (or, in her mind, her older brother), the one person who loved her without condition. I can only imagine how her entire world was turned upside down by my disappearance from her life.

And then there's me, stuck in a cycle of trying to piece together the truth and to make sense of a past that was so carefully manipulated, and still navigating the daily upheavals of trauma. The abuse that happened to us, that is the real crime, but it was my stepmother who twisted everything, and my father who denies and dismisses the truth, still regularly flying to the Philippines.

I wish I could go back – of course I do – but I can't. And the hardest part of healing is learning that no amount of wishing, imagining or rewriting in my head will ever undo what's been done. I can't go back to when my daughter was just a little girl in my arms. I can't relive those moments or rewrite the choices that were never truly mine to begin with. The past is fixed, and carrying its weight is something I'll live with forever. But what I've learned is that staying trapped in those imagined re-dos only takes me further from the one thing I can still shape: the future.

I can't change the years that have been stolen from us, but I can fight for justice – not just for me, but for her and for other children like us. I fight for the little girl whose life was forever altered in ways no child should ever have to experience. And I fight for the little boy I was – the one who had no voice, no way to escape, no way to stop what was happening.

If it weren't for the fact that one day I'll have to sit down with my daughter and explain that the woman she knows as her mother committed these unforgivable crimes, I think it's fair to say that I'd wish my stepmother a slow, excruciating fall into a vat of acid. But rather than hold onto that fantasy, all I can do now is hold onto the hope that one day, when the time is right, my daughter will know the truth and we will reconnect. She will know who I am – a father who never stopped loving her, who never stopped thinking about her, who never stopped wishing he could have been there to protect her. I hope she will read this one day, and understand that everything I did, even in my silence, was because I loved her with every ounce of my being.

TRANSFORMING YOUR PAIN INTO PURPOSE

Pain doesn't have to be a life sentence and it doesn't have to define you forever. I never thought I'd get to a place where I could genuinely say that. For years, I didn't even believe it was possible. When you're stuck in the aftermath of abuse, when you're tangled in the mess of your own mind, the idea of 'turning pain into purpose' can sound like a cruel joke. But somehow, slowly, something began to shift.

It wasn't magic. There was no moment of enlightenment where everything just clicked and made sense. It was more like sifting through a ton of rubble and, every so often, uncovering a small, unexpected piece of hope, then another, and another, until I realised that while I couldn't undo the past, I could shape what came next. Maybe not with a neat bow, but with meaning. With direction. With power.

Healing doesn't always look like a grand transformation. Sometimes it's as simple as getting out of bed on the days when the world feels far too heavy, or saying 'no' to Friday night drinks with your work colleagues without feeling guilty. It's allowing yourself to cry during your fifth rewatch of *Inside Out 2* without judgment. It's laughing at something genuinely funny, like when your brother walks straight into a glass door he thought was open. It's choosing to switch your phone off and run down to the beach for a dip in the ocean. It's speaking up when silence has been your default.

It's knowing that, despite what was modelled to you, you've chosen to be a gentle, safe presence for everyone in your life, and to choose partners who do the same. You learned a different lesson from the one they tried to teach you.

Healing lives in those small moments of strength. The quiet decisions to choose life, to keep moving forward, even when you don't feel like you have the energy. It's the resilience that emerges not from defeating the pain, but from learning to live alongside it, and still finding ways to grow.

That's what this book is about.

I wrote the book I wish I had when I first spoke out publicly. When I was filled with purpose but had no idea how to channel it. When I had a voice, but no clue how to use it. I wanted a resource that didn't just tell me to 'share my story' or 'speak my truth', but actually walked me through how to navigate systems designed to shut you out. How to turn a personal experience into something that could change laws, change lives or even just change your own sense of self-worth.

Each chapter in this book is a tool to do just that.

Each begins with a story, a real moment from my life that shaped me, challenged me or moved me forward. Then we'll unpack it. Not in a vague, motivational-quote kind of way, but in a real, practical way. I'll walk you through what I learned while campaigning for legislative change across Australia; the steps I took, how I continued to learn, to pick myself up, to keep persevering. The strategy behind moments that looked spontaneous, how I navigated media storms, the questions I asked myself when the stakes were high. How you can take what you've lived through and shape it into action and advocacy, into something that outlives you – or merely into a well-lived life, full of chosen family and wonderful experiences.

At the end of each chapter, there are prompts for you to reflect, to brainstorm and to take stock of what you've just read and apply it to your own life, your own cause, your own campaign. You'll be invited to map your own goals, shape your own message (whether you want to send it to your immediate circle or to the world) and identify your own next steps. This book isn't just something to read – it's something to use. But please only take what you're ready for. Everyone arrives at their own pace; some parts might speak to you now, others later, and some maybe not at all, and that's okay.

While this story is rooted in my own experiences as an activist and survivor of child sexual abuse, this book isn't only for survivors. It's for anyone who's been through something dark and found themselves asking, 'What now?' It's for people fighting for change in any area of injustice – climate, racial equity, disability rights, gender, mental health, housing, animal rights – whatever your cause, whatever your reason for picking up this book, you're welcome here. You're needed here.

This book is about turning the unspeakable, unfathomable and absolutely fucked parts of life into catalysts for something bigger. It's about taking your pain and using it as fuel not just for survival, but for change. Not just for you, but for others. Because when you start to rise from the ashes, you realise you're no longer just a consequence of what happened to you. You're what you do with it.

Chapter 1

THE WORDS YOU NEVER HAD THE CHANCE TO SAY

Have you ever been lying in bed at 2.15am, staring at the ceiling on an existential bender, replaying an argument from earlier that day and crafting the perfect one-liner that would've absolutely obliterated your opponent? If only time travel were real, right?

Or maybe you're in the shower the next morning, water running, with a full-blown courtroom fantasy playing out in your head, rehearsing line after line for a fight that ended eighteen hours ago, delivering closing arguments to the shampoo bottles like your entire dignity depends on it?

Or maybe you're driving to work, gripping the steering wheel like it personally offended you, rerunning that conversation with your ex and emotionally belting out a break-up ballad like you're auditioning for *Australian Idol* – except it's just you, your shitty almond latte and a 2014 Toyota Corolla with a *Live, Laugh, Love* pendant that feels wildly out of place swinging from the rearview mirror?

Yeah, we've all been there.

It's human nature: we bottle things up, keep it polite in the moment, then unleash the rage when we're alone and able to deliver an Oscar-worthy monologue to ourselves in the bathroom mirror. And that's fine when we're talking about a tiff with a friend or a passive-aggressive comment from your co-worker; but what happens when the thing you didn't say wasn't just an off-the-cuff clapback, but the truth about your pain? What happens when the words stuck in your throat are the ones you've been carrying for years? The ones too loaded, too complicated or too dangerous to speak out loud?

Whether your pain comes from living through systemic injustice, watching the climate crisis unfold, burning out in activism, being gaslit at work or home or simply never being taken seriously when you speak, we all carry the weight of unsaid words. And those words matter.

There's a concept often recommended in therapy known as Healing Through Unsent Letters where, after experiencing profound trauma or something that altered your life – whether that may be child sexual abuse, domestic violence, inequality, bullying or the heartbreak of a shattered marriage – a person writes a letter to the people who have hurt them. Not to send it, but to give themselves the chance to say the things they've held inside for so long; to give voice to words that were so cruelly stolen from them, without apology, interruption or shame.

Writing an unsent letter won't fix everything, but it can be the first honest conversation you've had with yourself in a long time. It might be the moment you stop running from your story and start owning it.

In life, and in activism, whether you're trying to change a

broken system, plan your way out of an abusive household, save our planet or hold a conglomerate to account, owning and using your voice is where it all begins.

The pain we feel doesn't always present itself in a way that's recognisable to others, or even to ourselves, and it certainly doesn't always have an easy-to-follow script. But no matter what it looks like, one thing always remains the same: the weight of unspoken words can be suffocating. Healing Through Unsent Letters is a method rooted in the belief that free expression has the power to lighten the unbearable weight we carry. And, especially for those of us who have known the tragedy of trauma, that weight can feel impossible to shake.

According to charity Trauma Research UK, this practice can be a profound step in the healing process. Writing an unsent letter can be a cathartic release, providing a sense of closure even when direct communication isn't possible. It allows us to confront our pain safely, without the fear of retaliation or further harm. The idea isn't to forgive, forget or move on, but to free ourselves from the silence that trauma demands. It's about regaining a sense of control over our own narrative.

Let's be honest: when you're buried under the crushing weight of trauma, the idea of 'healing through words' can feel like a frustrating, time-wasting exercise that seems impossible to even start. I used to think a pen and paper couldn't possibly compete with the scale of what I'd been through. It felt pointless, like being handed a teaspoon to bail water off the *Titanic*. But I'd tried everything else. Drinking until the memories blurred, working myself to exhaustion, hoping if I ran fast enough, I could outrun the past. Numbing the ache however I could – fast food, fleeting distractions, jumping from relationship to situationship and back again – anything to avoid sitting in it for too long. I told myself I was fine, that the worst was over. That if I ignored it long enough, maybe it would just go away.

But trauma does not work like that. It doesn't vanish after you give it the metaphorical middle finger, and it doesn't knock politely or ask for permission. It just barges through your mental door uninvited and is the worst housemate ever, throwing its shit all over the place, leaving dirty dishes in your mind and taking up more space than it has any right to. It rearranges your thoughts, leaves clutter everywhere, consumes all your energy and settles its bare ass on your mental couch. And no matter how many times you ask it to leave, it will continue making itself comfortable while you try to get on with your life.

Trauma takes up residence in your body, too. It hides in the tension of your shoulders, the tightness in your chest, the anxiety that coils around your stomach like a Burmese python with its prey, squeezing tighter with every breath. It weaves through your DNA, embedding itself so deeply that it starts to feel like a part of who you are – like a shadow that follows you around, no matter how far you try to run from it. After a while, you don't even know who you were before it, or who you might have been without it. The conditioning becomes so deeply wired into you that it feels impossible to separate yourself from it, and that's what makes the shift so hard to begin. Trauma has a way of smudging the edges of who you are, until you're not quite sure where your personality ends and the pain begins.

And just when you think you've made it out – that you've healed, moved on, patched yourself back together – something small can pull you right back in. A comment. A look. A raised voice. Suddenly, you're fawning to keep the peace, freezing mid-sentence, unable to advocate for yourself in a conversation that shouldn't feel threatening. The past floods the present in an instant, and you realise those old survival instincts never really left; they were just waiting.

That's the quiet, cunning nature of trauma – it doesn't announce its return. It just shows up, slips inside and sits quietly in the corner … until you notice your hands shaking again.

After doing a hell of a lot of work on myself, I've realised that the words I never said actually lived inside me for years, quietly gnawing away, bit by bit, constantly reminding me that silence always comes at a cost. You'd be surprised how often survivors of abuse who speak out are asked, 'Why didn't you say something sooner?' It's one of those questions that gets tossed around, as if it's just innocent curiosity and isn't soaked in judgment and part of a larger, harmful narrative that quietly suggests it's on us, the victims of these destructive crimes, to prevent our own abuse. That if we didn't speak up the moment it happened, it must not have been 'that bad'; as if silence is proof of consent, as if the absence of a scream is the absence of pain. As if trauma is supposed to arrive with perfect clarity and instant vocabulary instead of confusion, fear, shame and a desperate need to feel safe. It is a mindset that ignores everything we know about survival, reducing an entire human experience to a reaction time, like we were supposed to hit some imaginary stopwatch to prove our suffering. It's a narrative that fuels silence and blames the survivor.

According to the Final Report of Australia's Royal Commission into Institutional Responses to Child Sexual Abuse – initiated by Prime Minister Julia Gillard – it takes victim–survivors an average of twenty-four years to disclose their abuse. Let that sink in. *Twenty-four years.* That's not because we're slow, or unsure, or wake up one day to talk about it on a whim. It's because silence isn't failure; it's a survival strategy.

When the person who abused you is someone you're supposed to trust, someone who convinces you that you're complicit – that you wanted it, you asked for it, you'd ruin everything if you told – speaking out doesn't feel brave so much as impossible. Shame becomes a second skin. Fear becomes a compass dictating your every move. So you carry the burden quietly, convinced that your pain is something to be endured, and never, ever shared.

This is how my years of convincing myself that my voice didn't matter played out. I was certain that the damage had already been done, and no amount of words could change that.

But here's what I've come to realise: speaking, even if it's only to a blank page, is a rebellion. A refusal to let the pain dictate the rest of my life. It was a way of telling my abuser: *I'm still here. My story deserves to be told. You don't get to hold this over me anymore.* Silence keeps us stuck, and I'm done being stuck. Aren't you?

Vulnerability is one of the most powerful and courageous things we have as human beings, and when we see someone else choose it – when we witness someone open themselves up – it does something truly special. It gives us permission to do the same, like dominos, falling one after the other. That's how healing spreads and change begins.

THIS IS WHERE YOUR STORY BEGINS

Originally, this chapter was going to include a very personal letter addressed to Mr and Mrs Cunty McFuckface of Cuntworthington, also known as my father and stepmother. They were the first people I ever directed this exercise toward. I wrote those letters long before I ever stood on a stage, gave a media interview or knew what it meant to organise a national campaign. I wasn't an 'activist', I was just a kid with years of pain living in my chest and no idea how to let it out. I thought including those letters here might help someone feel seen; maybe they'd resonate with the quiet rage, or the grief, or the shame. Or the sense that if only you could say what's inside you, something might finally shift. I had hoped my words might give someone else permission to write their own.

For legal reasons, I have been told that I can't include those letters here. And, to be honest, that felt like a gut-punch. Another hit from a system that still finds ways to silence survivors, that told me, once again, that my voice was too dangerous. A system that always seems to protect the wrong people.

After I sat with it and the sting wore off, I realised something far more powerful: maybe this chapter was never meant to be about my letters.

It's about yours.

Because what I needed to say doesn't matter as much as you saying what you need to say – to whoever or whatever needs to hear it. And I'm not just talking to survivors of child sexual abuse like me. I'm talking to anyone who's grieving, or raging, or ready to change something within our society that has gone on far too long.

Maybe the person you need to write to is a parent who never believed you. Or a boss who humiliated you. Or a doctor who dismissed your pain. Maybe it's a friend who betrayed you. A partner who broke something sacred. A teacher who made you feel small. A government that won't act. A system that let you down.

Or maybe, the person you need to write to is yourself.

No matter what the cause, I've found the fight almost always begins with personal pain. With something that wasn't okay, a wound that never quite healed. And when you don't give yourself space to acknowledge that wound, it can quietly dictate everything that follows.

So before you jump into action – before you launch your movement or join someone else's – I want to offer you this, the first tool in your activist kit: write the letter you never got to write.

The one you've been carrying in your body for years – the one that sits in your chest like a brick and makes your throat close up when you try to speak.

You don't need to send it. You don't need to share it, or even to keep it. You just need to say it. *For you.*

If you want to move forward with clarity, courage and your whole heart, you have to name what hurt you. You have to make space for your voice, even if it shakes. Especially if it shakes. That's what this chapter is about: reclaiming your story before the world tries to shape it for you. Putting it on the page before it explodes in your chest. Making room for truth before it rots into resentment.

Let it be messy. Let it be angry. Let it be petty. Let it be brilliant. Let it be painful. Let it be honest. This is not about writing something perfect; it's about writing something true.

Use a notebook, or the Notes app in your phone, or scribble it on a napkin if you have to.

This is yours.

If you're stuck and don't know where to begin, use the following questions as starting points. You don't need to answer all of them. Just pick one, and begin.

- Who do you need to write to, and why now?
- What's one thing you wish they knew?
- What did they take from you?
- What did you lose because of what happened?
- What were you too afraid to say at the time?
- What would it feel like to finally say it?
- What did you need, that you never got?
- What would you say to your younger self in that moment?
- What has this pain taught you – and what are you ready to let go of?
- What belief about yourself are you no longer willing to carry?
- What do you still believe in, despite everything?
- What kind of world would you rather build?

THIS IS WHAT COURAGE LOOKS LIKE

Congratulations.

Seriously. If you just wrote your letter – even part of it – that's a monumental step. It doesn't matter if it was one line or an entire notebook, whether you sobbed through it or stared at a blank page until something finally came out, you did something incredibly brave. You chose to stop bottling it up. You chose to face something you've been carrying alone. And that matters.

Now, I want to be really clear: this isn't the start of your campaign. This is the moment just before. It's the groundwork, the clearing of the debris so that something real – something meaningful and powerful and entirely yours – can start to take shape.

It's that breath you take before stepping onto the stage, or the pause before the protest, or when you realise something has triggered your old coping mechanisms. The moment where you reclaim your voice, not to prove a point or win anyone over, but because you deserve to hear yourself again without editing yourself down to be more palatable. Because real, lasting change always begins with truth. And before you try to shift the world around you, it helps to get honest about the world inside you. That's what this letter is: not a performance or strategy, but an acknowledgement of the thing that once made you go quiet – and your decision to speak anyway.

You've survived silence, and now you've written the thing you weren't meant to write.

That is no small thing.

So use your blank pages however you need to. Scribble. Rip it out of your notebook. Revisit it later. Or don't. There are no rules here. This isn't about being polished or perfect – it's about being authentic, and loosening the grip that silence had on you. Once you've reclaimed that space inside yourself, you're in a much stronger position to step into what comes next.

Because this is where you start to find your voice again.

Chapter 2

BUILD YOUR SUPPORT NETWORK

Have you ever told yourself, 'I'm fine,' so many times that you almost started to believe it – even when, deep down, you knew you absolutely weren't?

You go to work. You catch up with friends. You laugh at things that are actually funny. You post a photo online, reply to a message, order a coffee. On the outside, everything looks 'normal' – maybe even good. But underneath, there's a part that's not fine, screaming for someone to notice that something's not right. You hold that something in for so long that it starts to feel like part of your anatomy, like a knot in your stomach that never quite untangles. Like a pair of shoes that are one size too small, but you've convinced yourself they fit just fine. Like every breath comes with the question, 'Is it safe to exhale yet?'

That was me.

For years, I silently pretended that I was okay while carrying a truth that felt too big for my chest. I thought keeping it all inside and staying silent made me resilient. A 'real man'. I thought staying busy would make it all go away, that if I just kept moving – smiling, working, living – maybe the anger I was feeling would eventually dissolve and become a distant memory. But the truth has a way of finding its voice especially when it's been silenced for too long.

Years passed while my father kept getting on planes to the Philippines to see my stepmother, the woman I had told him had sexually abused me, well beyond the one-off moment he saw firsthand. He still does it to this day. I cannot comprehend why. The only explanations that seem remotely plausible are complete denial, or an inability to overcome his own ego and take accountability for the role he played. This is my father, the man who was supposed to protect me, who was supposed to believe me. Surely that wasn't asking too much?

Yet, even after all the hurt my stepmother caused, after all the chances I gave him to stand by me, he still chose her.

I felt like a kettle left to boil too long – steam building, pressure rising, the whistle of pain I could no longer mute. I had to let it out. Not for attention or shock value, but for validation. I needed someone – anyone – to hear my story and say, *I believe you. That wasn't your fault.* I wasn't looking for applause. I was looking for air.

On 31 March 2022, I sat alone in my tiny studio apartment, the sterile glow of my phone camera casting shadows across my face, and hit record. I remembered something Brené Brown once said: courage, in its original form, meant 'to share the story of who you are with your whole heart'. That was what I needed to do. Not just to speak, but to speak from the centre of my chest, to give my pain a voice before it swallowed me whole.

'My name is Harrison James,' I said, 'and I am a survivor.'

This was the first time I said the words out loud without holding back to anyone beyond my mum or my therapist, and this time, I was saying them to anyone who would listen. Eleven minutes of raw, unfiltered truth poured out of me. I wasn't polished. I wasn't rehearsed. I wasn't trying to say everything perfectly – I was just trying to say *something*, to leach the poison from my system. And when I finally pressed *post* on that video, a complex concoction of fear and liberation washed over me. There was no turning back now. Even though my heart was still thudding like a drum in my chest, for the first time in years, I could breathe. I couldn't help but wonder if anyone would care. Would I be met with support, or with doubt and stigma?

What happened in the days and weeks that followed exceeded every expectation. I had 400 followers on Instagram at the time, and the video was viewed over 60,000 times – a number I could hardly fathom. Tens of thousands of eyes were on my story, on me. More overwhelming than the view count, though, were the responses. My inbox was filled with hundreds of messages from people all over the country (and even abroad) who saw the video and felt compelled to reach out. Many were survivors of sexual abuse themselves. Strangers – women, men, young and old – wrote to say 'me too', sharing pieces of their own stories of abuse and survival. Some had never told a soul before seeing my video, but now they found the courage to speak, even if it was just in a private message. They wrote things like, *Your video made me feel less alone* and *I've lived with this secret for decades, but seeing you speak out gives me hope I can heal.*

As for my father, there was a response, but far from the one I needed. What came back to me, through an unnamed source, wasn't remorse or reflection; it was fury. A threat to 'watch my back' when walking in public. And while I won't say more than that here, I will say this: his reaction didn't matter as much as I thought it would. Because what stayed with me – what actually changed me – wasn't his anger. It was the hundreds of strangers who wrote to share their stories, and their courage and willingness to speak, sometimes for the very first time, which made me realise I was no longer alone.

I sat on my bed reading these replies with tears in my eyes. I cried for their pain, and I cried for my own younger self who had felt so alone, thinking no one could possibly understand. The isolation was debilitating, but now I knew, in the most undeniable way, that I was not alone. By exposing my wounds, I had connected with a vast, unseen community of survivors. It was as if by shining a light on my darkness, others found a pathway to step out of their own shadows.

In those early days after the video, I hardly slept, not because of nightmares (though those still came, sometimes) but because of the adrenaline and emotion of it all. I tried to respond to every single person who wrote to me. It felt like a sacred trust; if someone was brave enough to share their story with me, I wanted to honour that by acknowledging them. The idea that my eleven-minute video – just me, sitting in my living room with my heart in my throat, telling the ugly truth – could give another survivor the courage to finally speak out … it was both humbling and profoundly affirming.

Brené Brown was right: telling my story did become part of someone else's survival guide.

Not all responses were positive, of course. This is the internet, after all, and when you speak publicly about childhood sexual abuse, especially as a young man, you're bound to attract a certain kind of cruelty. Some people lash out at what they don't understand. A few comments were dismissive or accusatory – the usual toxic myths like, *Why didn't you fight back?* or *This guy lived the dream!* or *Real-life Stifler's mum!* (a reference to the *American Pie* film series from the early 2000s). And the one I see most: 'Boys can't be abused by women without wanting it.' That last one stings more than I can explain. It echoes one of the oldest, most damaging lies about victims: that we're somehow complicit or, worse, 'lucky'. I had braced myself for responses like these, but that didn't make them hurt any less. I still get comments like that to this day – no matter how many times I speak out, or how many people publicly support the work I do. There are always a few who show up in my inbox or under a post with some variation of, *You should've enjoyed it* or *You're just trying to get attention*. It's exhausting, but I've learned to stop internalising their ignorance and start recognising it for what it is: not a reflection of me, but of them.

And for every one nasty comment, there were dozens of kind ones. Masses of people saw my video and said, 'Thank you,' or 'I've never told anyone this before, but me too.' And that made all the difference.

That video marked the end of one chapter of my life – the chapter of silent suffering – and the beginning of a new one. I had broken my personal silence in a very public way and laid a foundation of honesty on which I hoped to build something meaningful. At the time, I didn't fully know what that would be. I just knew I couldn't stop at telling my story – I had to do something. I summarised my newfound philosophy in one of my replies to a commenter: *Whether you heal in silence or with a megaphone is up to you – I've decided to use a megaphone.*

Telling the truth was step one. Now I felt an overwhelming responsibility to use my voice to make a difference. I was determined that my pain would have a purpose beyond my own healing. I wanted to help prevent this horror from happening to other kids or, at the very least, to support survivors so they never feel as alone as I once did.

In the aftermath, everything shifted. I was no longer just that young guy from the internet with a painful past; I had become Harrison James, the survivor who speaks truth to power. People in the survivor community started recognising my name. Invitations for speaking gigs began rolling in – community town halls, trauma conferences, university lectures, podcasts. It was a whirlwind. All those years of classes as a kid at the National Institute of Dramatic Art finally started to pay off, as well as the guidance from my incredibly generous speaking coach, Chris Whitnall. I was being asked to speak across the country and sit on panels alongside psychologists and social workers as 'the lived-experience voice'. I can't count how many times I uttered the statistic from the Australian Child Maltreatment Study – that in Australia, one in three girls and one in five boys are sexually abused before their eighteenth birthday – and saw shock ripple through audiences, who had no idea the number was so high.

I learned to harness my nerves and speak from the heart, and what I found – again and again – was that people connected more deeply when I didn't read from a script or try to be polished. When I admitted I was scared, or when I said, 'I don't have all the answers,' or I let the emotion break through my voice, those were the moments that landed. That's when people leaned in – not because I was perfect, but because I was real. I'll speak more about this in Chapter 7. For now, just know that honesty speaks louder than perfection ever could.

Part of me felt like an impostor – me, barely in my twenties and with no formal qualifications in this area being looked to as some kind of expert? But another part of me – the part that had promised to make my pain matter – knew I had to step up. I reminded myself: *You wanted to make a difference. This is how it begins.*

I even launched my own clothing line: Fuck Injustice. The name alone said everything – bold, unapologetic and impossible to ignore. It was raw pain turned into wearable protest. I channelled everything I was feeling into product-based advocacy, designing bright, punchy slogans that demanded attention and invited conversation.

Why clothing? Because I knew not everyone would sit through an eleven-minute video about child sexual abuse or show up to a town hall meeting, but they'd notice a statement on a shirt walking down the street. If someone saw *Fuck Injustice* across my chest and asked, 'What's that about?', there was an opening, a conversation that never would've happened otherwise. A colourful cap at the checkout line in the grocery store. A hoodie worn while studying in the university library. A sticker slapped on a water bottle or the back of a laptop. It was advocacy in the wild, the kind that doesn't need a podium or a press release to make an impact. Just people going about their lives, wearing their values out loud. That, to me, is advocacy at its best – unexpected, everyday and boldly impossible to ignore.

I've always loved graphic design and I used to spend hours

drawing cartoons as a kid (and yes, one of my party tricks is drawing Donald Duck in under thirty seconds – ask me if we ever meet). I launched the brand with a simple online store and a small batch of hats, shirts and hoodies. They sold out quickly. What moved me most wasn't the sales, but the messages that followed. Survivors sending selfies in their hoodies, standing tall. One person from Melbourne sent me a picture and said, *Every time I wear this, I feel proud of surviving and standing up.* It was beautiful.

I opened my inbox to an invitation to become an ambassador for Polished Man, a global campaign that encourages men (and, really, everyone) to paint one fingernail during October to raise awareness about violence against children. The painted nail is a conversation starter, symbolising the one in five children who experience violence in their lifetime.

The word 'ambassador' didn't feel like it belonged to someone like me. That title belonged to celebrities and household names they already had on board – people like Zac Efron, Kelly Slater, Chris Hemsworth. They had fucking *Thor* painting a nail, and now they wanted me?

I sat there, rereading the email, half-laughing, but once I recovered from the shock, it felt like validation. That the path I was walking actually meant something, and my voice could carry weight. That someone, somewhere, believed I had something to offer.

Throughout my first year of advocacy in 2022, I juggled it all – the speaking gigs, the media appearances, the painted nail for Polished Man, the bold slogans of my merch line – but beneath it all, I knew where I wanted this to go. From the very beginning, my heart was set on something bigger than awareness: legislative change. I didn't want to just talk about the problem; I wanted to help fix the laws that were actively failing survivors.

I wasn't naive. I knew I couldn't just walk into parliament and expect a red-carpet welcome. I needed to build credibility first, to show I was serious. I needed patience, strategy and connections.

It often felt isolating. After a talk or a live interview, I'd go home to my empty apartment. No debriefs, no team huddles, no one to toast the little wins with. I had amazing mentors and supportive friends, but no one to walk the path with me. And the work was heavy: listening to people's stories and retelling my own. There were nights I'd lie awake, wondering how much more I could carry. As much as I respected other advocates paving their own way, I knew I didn't want to do this alone. I longed for someone to build with, someone who understood it from the inside out. A teammate who'd call it 'our mission'. Someone I could message at 1am when an idea hit and say, *Hey, hear me out on this …*

And then, just when I needed it most, someone showed up. Not God – I'm still waiting on his reply – but close enough. In August 2022, I was mindlessly scrolling through Instagram one morning, half-awake and catching up on notifications. My inbox was the usual chaotic mix – supportive messages from strangers, the occasional troll and a spam link offering what was definitely a fake brand collaboration with a protein shake company I'd never heard of, promising to make me the face of 'Whey 2 Sexy.' But one new DM caught my eye, from someone named Jarad Grice. I didn't recognise the name, but the preview read:

Hey Harrison, just wanted to congratulate you on becoming a Polished Man ambassador …

I clicked it open.

The message was warm, thoughtful and longer than I expected. Jarad introduced himself as a fellow survivor and advocate. He wrote that he'd been following my journey since I'd posted my video in March and that he was genuinely moved by how I was so young and using my voice. He mentioned that he too was an ambassador for the Polished Man campaign, and seeing another male survivor representing the cause felt meaningful to him. *We need more of it, mate*, he wrote.

I learned that Jarad was in his forties, lived only about half an hour away from me, was an architect by trade and that outside of work, he volunteered with a survivor organisation called Survivors and Mates Support Network (SAMSN). He said he'd only begun publicly speaking about his own experience in recent years, and that seeing people like me speak up gave him hope. He signed off with, *If you ever want to chat or need support, I'm here. It's always good to connect with someone who gets it. Proud of what you're doing – keep it up.*

As I sat staring at my phone, a quiet kind of gratitude settled in my chest. Here was someone I didn't know – but somehow, I did. A brother-in-survival. Someone who understood the terrain I was walking, because he'd walked it too. And he wasn't asking for anything. He was just reaching out with respect, solidarity and that rare kind of sincerity that feels like someone gently placing a hand on your shoulder without needing to say a word.

I replied quickly, thanking him for the message and for the work he was doing. I told him I was curious to hear more about his story, and I appreciated that he'd been following mine.

From there, the conversation flowed. Over the next few days, we volleyed messages back and forth like old mates catching up. He told me his story in fragments: the abuse happened when he was just a kid by a trusted neighbour. He didn't tell anyone until he was in his late teens, when the pressure of silence became unbearable. Years later, he even tried to seek justice through the courts, but the trial ended in a hung jury and his perpetrator walked free. *It was brutal*, he wrote. *But even just telling my story out loud in that setting … it gave me a piece of power back.* That stuck with me. I knew exactly what he meant.

Eventually, we agreed to meet up in person at the Dolphin Hotel in Surry Hills, a laid-back, slightly artsy place with exposed brick, soft lighting and the kind of ambient hum that makes serious conversations feel just a bit easier – everything an architect like Jarad would appreciate.

I was sitting by the window, watching the world go by with a schooner in hand, when I spotted him walking toward the pub. As he reached the entrance, he looked around until our eyes met. I stood and he greeted me with a hug like we'd known each other for years, which caught me off guard in the best possible way. Lots of blokes on a first meeting default to a simple handshake; not Jarad. From the get-go, he wasn't interested in posturing – he was just real.

We sat down, ordered a round, and just talked. About life, about advocacy, about what it means to be a man who carries this kind of pain. He asked how I was holding up – not the surface-level 'how are you?' but the kind that lands. I told him honestly: some days, I was running on purpose and adrenaline. Other days, the weight of it all flattened me.

We shared stories we hadn't told many people. The guilt. The shame. The confusion. That quiet, desperate longing for someone – anyone – to have stepped in. We spoke about how hard it is to explain what it feels like to be a young boy who's been sexually abused. The way the world expects strength from you, even when your childhood has been torn apart. The twisted belief that maybe you wanted it, maybe you allowed it, maybe it was somehow your fault, and the years it takes to unlearn that kind of thinking and conditioning. The way it creeps into every corner of your self-worth.

Jarad listened, really listened. He didn't interrupt, didn't rush to reassure me. He just nodded along, not with pity, but with knowing. When he spoke, it was with a calmness that comes from having walked through fire and come out the other side.

As the conversation dipped into a pause, I felt it rise up in me – that urge to pursue something bigger than myself. It had been sitting in my chest since I'd begun in advocacy just months earlier. An intense pull toward something beyond awareness, beyond storytelling. The drive to change laws that had failed people like us. It had lingered in the background of everything I'd done, waiting for the right moment, the right person, the right table at the right pub. And now, I had an idea to share with Jarad.

I told him about something in the legal system that didn't right with me. Something that had quietly haunted me since the day I found out that my father, during a court case where he was found guilty of perpetrating domestic violence against my mum, had used good character references to try to soften his sentence. It was soul-crushing, not just because of what he'd done, but because even after being held accountable in a courtroom, he was still allowed to bring in a parade of people – mainly colleagues and friends – who stood up and vouched for what a 'great bloke' he was. As if being charming or generous in other parts of your life could somehow cancel out the fact that you've inflicted violence on your own family. That injustice stayed with me for years, festering. And once I began advocacy, it started morphing into a sharper question: if this is allowed in domestic violence cases, is it happening in child sexual abuse cases too? So I looked it up. And when I realised the answer was yes, I felt sick.

I told Jarad everything. How my dad had used that loophole, how I couldn't believe it was still a standard legal practice, a gap in the law big enough to drive a semitrailer through. In practice, nearly every offender had character references or letters tendered during their sentencing hearing, because, of course, they typically were seen as upstanding citizens – that's how they accessed victims in the first place. I told him how I'd been carrying this idea for months: that maybe someone should push to remove good character references from being used in child sexual abuse sentencing. Because how could you possibly be of good character if you've raped a child? It was a slap in the face to every survivor who had to sit in a courtroom and listen to their abuser be publicly praised.

Jarad didn't flinch. He just nodded, with the kind of look only another survivor could give – equal parts anger, recognition and readiness. In that moment, I wasn't just venting; I was laying the groundwork for something bigger. And, I could feel in my gut, so was he. That was the moment something clicked, and the energy shifted. This wasn't just a conversation between two survivors anymore. This was the beginning of a movement. And we both knew it.

I went home that night with my head buzzing, partly from ideas, partly from the kind of disbelief that settles in after meeting someone and clicking so deeply, it almost feels fated. Jarad Grice had walked into my life as a stranger in my DMs, and had become a trusted friend and comrade-in-arms. In the weeks following our meeting at the Dolphin, we were in constant contact. It felt like we'd lit a match, and neither of us wanted to let the flame die out. We began catching up regularly, mapping out the early blueprint of what would become our campaign to abolish good character references in child sexual abuse sentencing. We texted and called nearly every day, quickly becoming fixtures in each other's lives.

We started talking strategy. If we were going to do this, how would we even begin? Changing a law wasn't a small feat. We needed a game plan. Should we start a petition? Meet with politicians? Launch a social media campaign to build public support? Seek legal advice? We agreed that we would likely need to do all of the above. I mentioned a few lawyers I knew of who might be able to help us figure out the next steps – people who could provide honest, strategic advice. Jarad, ever measured and pragmatic, agreed it was worth reaching out. I jotted a note in my phone before the thought slipped away.

Then came the moment every campaign needs – the naming. We needed something sharp. A rallying cry. A hashtag that could live in people's minds. A phrase that captured the heart of the issue and refused to let go. We threw around ideas: No Good Reference? Not punchy enough. No Relevance? Too vague. They Shouldn't Carry So Much Weight? Way too long.

We kept circling the same truth: these references shouldn't matter. They're irrelevant to the crime. That word kept bouncing back and forth between us. Irrelevant. *Irrelevant.* Until, finally, the right phrase surfaced between us, like it had been sitting there all along: *Your Reference Ain't Relevant*. We both paused, the same realisation landing at once. That was it. Blunt. Unapologetic. Clear. Direct. It had attitude. It told the whole story in five words, no explanation needed. It didn't just name the injustice; it challenged it.

It was the spark. Naming it gave the idea shape and, suddenly, the weight we'd been carrying had somewhere to land and a purpose to anchor it. The campaign had a name and now, we had our mission.

After we christened our cause, I felt excited. This wasn't just about giving ourselves a banner to rally under; it was about defining why we were fighting in the first place. The more we talked it through, the clearer it became that our mission was necessary in ways we hadn't fully articulated until that moment. We weren't just launching a campaign, we were taking a stand against a deep-rooted societal injustice that we had both lived through.

Why was this campaign so important? Because we knew that a predator's so-called good character was often the cloak that allowed them to prey. Jarad and I had seen it firsthand: the beloved footy coach, the family doctor, the scout leader, the school principal, the swim instructor, the dad of a friend who always offers a lift home – those were the masks survivors knew abusers wore. Their public kindness wasn't a redeeming trait; it was a tactic that enabled their crimes. It earned them trust, access and the benefit of doubt.

I was sixteen when I found out who had stood up in court to vouch for my abusive father's so-called good character. People who had shared dinner with us, who had seen the bruises and knew what he was capable of – or, at the very least, knew enough to suspect. These were the same people who looked the other way when my Mum was being hurt. These same ones, who chose silence when we needed protection, and used their voices not to seek justice, but to defend him and call him an upstanding man.

Their glowing words helped him escape consequences. Their references weren't just character assessments; they were another form of betrayal.

I learned a hard truth: an abuser's public reputation often shields their private monstrosity. For predators, the 'good person' persona is intentional. It lets them get close to children and makes others say, 'There's no way he'd never do something like that,' even when he did.

As we refined our mission, Jarad and I kept returning to a phrase: 'Prevention, not just reaction'. It might seem odd, since we were talking about sentencing, something that comes after an offender has been found unequivocally guilty of a crime. How could that be about prevention? But that idea became our guiding philosophy in several ways. First, even a post-crime measure can prevent further harm. Ending the practice of praising an abuser's good character in court would prevent the re-traumatisation of survivors. No survivor should have to sit there and listen as their abuser is lauded as a great person. Stopping that practice was an act of prevention in that it kept new psychological wounds from opening in a place meant for justice.

Taking it a step further, eliminating these testimonials would prevent abusers from leveraging their good standing to escape accountability. It would close a loophole a lot of offenders counted on. Predators groom not only their victims, but everyone around them, cultivating respect so that if caught, people will rally to their defence. My stepmother did exactly that. She fooled my mother, my grandmother and the rest of my support system into believing she was a safe person – someone trustworthy enough to care for a thirteen-year-old boy. She built that image carefully and strategically. Her good character wasn't incidental; it was calculated. And when the abuse happened, the trust she had cultivated made it harder to believe, harder to speak out against and harder to escape.

These offenders don't just violate our bodies – they violate the trust of others, weaponising the very relationships that should offer protection. Take away the reward of a reduced sentence for 'good character' and you remove one incentive for that manipulative strategy. Even if it stops only one predator from thinking they can hide behind a good name, that prevention is worth it.

Building on that logic, we understood that our reform could ripple outward, helping prevent abuse on a larger scale by shifting culture and awareness. Changing a law sparks conversations. Abolishing character references would shine a light on how predators groom communities with good deeds and smiles. We wanted everyone – parents, teachers, neighbours – to understand that just because someone is kind in public doesn't mean they aren't capable of terrible harm. If communities become wiser to that tactic, they might spot red flags earlier, or at least not jump to defend an abuser just because 'he's such a good guy'. It could aid prevention by educating people and changing attitudes.

With these ideas clear, defined and outlined, we laid out three core goals for *#YourReferenceAintRelevant*:

- First, fight to change the law and abolish good character references in child sexual abuse sentencing.
- Second, educate the legal community and the public about why this change is necessary. Some people still believe letters attesting to an offender's character is a fair part of the sentencing process. We had to show how these glowing statements mislead justice and wound survivors. We needed to speak out in the media, gather survivor testimonies and meet with anyone who would listen – all to drive home one message: in cases of abuse, an offender's good reputation is often a carefully crafted lie.
- Third, empower survivors by making courtrooms centre their pain and truth rather than an abuser's accolades. We imagined a courtroom where what happened to the victim, once proven, is the focus, not how many friends the offender has. Survivors should never have to watch their abuser be praised in the place meant for justice. If even one survivor feels more validated because the abuser's reputation isn't paraded to overshadow their suffering, that's a victory.

We knew that even if we won this reform, it wouldn't fix everything wrong with the legal system. Child sexual abuse is complex and widespread; no single change to the law will end it or heal every hurt. We had no illusions that banning character references would stop all predators or make courts perfect. But this reform mattered because it was clear and achievable. In a landscape of countless needed changes, here was one concrete, practical step forward.

I thought of it like removing one toxic brick from a wall: by itself, it doesn't topple the structure, but it does weaken it. Removing character references would weaken the fortress offenders hide in. It would send a signal that our justice system is evolving.

While we sharpened our public mission, something equally important was happening between us. I was discovering the power of partnership in advocacy. Jarad stood beside me not just as a co-campaigner but as a true friend. As our movement gained momentum, our friendship deepened. We'd talk strategy for hours, then share our fears and hopes. In between drafting petitions and making calls, we checked in on each other's wellbeing. We asked each other how we were *really* doing, just as often as we asked what was next on the agenda. He listened without judgment on my sleepless nights; I sat with him through his heavy days. We became each other's support system, each holding the other up. Jarad's steady presence provided me with feelings of safety and understanding. When things got overwhelming, his practical advice cut through the noise and helped me refocus. Sometimes, even just a short message from him was enough to remind me I wasn't doing this alone. Those small acts of care healed parts of me I hadn't realised were still raw. He filled a void with genuine friendship and trust.

I learned to be there for him, too. For all his strength, Jarad had days when the weight of our fight and his past pressed him down. When red tape stalled our progress or a reminder of his trauma resurfaced, I tried to return the comfort he gave me. I'd remind him how far we'd come or show him a thank-you message we had received from a fellow survivor. After one major setback, I reminded him of what we had already achieved and assured him we would get through this, and watched a bit of hope return to his face. It hit me then that two wounded people really can help heal each other. By lifting him up, I was also lifting myself.

Our friendship became the bedrock of the campaign. I often think that bond was our first victory – the one that made all the others possible. We turned what could have been a lonely fight into a shared journey. When one of us grew weary, the other picked up the slack; when one doubted, the other kept the faith. We celebrated each small win together and steadied each other through setbacks. Crucially, we never lost hope at the same time. One of us could always remind the other why we started. In that way, we kept each other's fire burning, even when strong winds of doubt blew. And when the victories did come, they were sweeter for it because someone who truly understood it was right there beside me.

This journey taught me one of the most important lessons about activism – and it's something I come back to again and again: it starts with people. Every law that's changed, every headline that's run, every ripple of impact I've made all began with a conversation. A relationship. A moment of connection. Advocacy isn't about a sleek logo or an extravagant launch event; it begins with finding someone to build with. Someone who shares your fire but also steadies your hand when the flames rage. The causes we fight for are heavy and can crush you if you try to carry them alone. That's why building a support system is essential. Advocacy is a team sport, even if the team is just two people. Before our campaign had a website or a social media strategy, it had us – front and centre. People connected to our goal because of our stories. And that made all the difference.

Looking back, I realise now that our campaign's mission and our friendship's journey were never separate threads; they were one and the same. Our fight for legal reform was fuelled by personal pain, yes, but it was sustained by the kind of quiet, consistent support that only comes when you feel truly understood by someone else. Someone who's walked where you've walked, and who doesn't flinch when the truth gets too heavy. Together, we turned trauma into purpose, and isolation into solidarity.

This work is hard. It will break your heart over and over. It will test your stamina, your voice, your belief in systems and in people. But with the right person beside you – someone who sees the world through a similar lens, who steadies you when you lose hope and who pushes with you, not just beside you – the weight becomes bearable. The mission becomes a movement.

BUILDING SUPPORT AROUND YOU, AND CONSIDERATIONS BEFORE GOING PUBLIC

I have lost friends throughout the years who didn't want to 'pick sides' between me and my dad. People who said they loved us both. Family members who stayed neutral – as if neutrality was compassion.

Child sexual abuse has a way of making people turn a blind eye. They don't want to look, or believe it could be true. People tell themselves it's too complex, too messy, too sad, so they pretend it didn't happen – or water it down so it doesn't seem so bad.

When you go public, you confront people with the truth they've tried so hard to avoid, and not everyone reacts with empathy. Some will silence you. Some will attack you. Some will disappear. That loss can be brutal, especially when it's the people you thought would stay.

It's not just personal fallout; the legal risks are real too. In Australia, survivors who speak publicly about abuse, even when telling the truth, have been sued for defamation by their alleged abusers, usually as an intimidation tactic. While legal outcomes vary, being dragged into a courtroom can be traumatic and expensive.

That's why it's so important to protect yourself before sharing your story publicly. It's so important to understand that you do not owe anyone your story. Not yet. Not ever, if you don't want to.

I cannot thank Jarad enough. For showing up, and for staying in it with me. For being the person who believed in me when I'd gone so long without it. For turning an Instagram message into a friendship, and a friendship into a force for change. Who would've thought, sitting in that pub together, that we were about to launch a national movement?

CONSIDERING GOING PUBLIC?

Whether or not you choose to share your story with the media, the decision is deeply personal – and powerful. If you're thinking about going public, take a moment to check in with yourself first. Grab a pen, and answer the following questions seriously and honestly:

If you were to speak publicly – on camera, in a headline or on a podcast – what part of your story would feel the riskiest to say out loud? And is that the part that still hurts the most?

If you could say one sentence to the entire country – unfiltered, uninterrupted – what would it be? What do you need people to understand about what happened to you?

If your story became a headline tomorrow, what change would you hope it sparked – in law, in culture, in someone else's life?

Now list every way that message could be shared – and don't worry, you don't have to do them all. The checklist below is just to give you some ideas. Tick off anything that feels doable, exciting or worth considering. Choose what works for you.

There are a few blank lines at the end for you to add any other creative ways you might want to share your message:

- Podcasts
- Writing (essays, books, articles, poetry, Substack)

- Art or illustration
- Social media (reels, TikToks, Threads, tweets)
- Merch, clothing, patches, stickers
- Speaking or education
- Peer support or community-building
- Photography or short film
- Protests or grassroots campaigns
- Storytelling events
- Workshops
- ______________________________
- ______________________________
- ______________________________
- ______________________________
- ______________________________

You don't have to pick just one – and you don't have to do it today. But, as this list proves, there are so many ways to begin.

BUILDING A SUPPORT NETWORK, ONE PERSON AT A TIME

You don't need a detailed campaign plan before you start reaching out to people. You don't even need to be planning a campaign at all. Maybe you're not trying to change laws or start a movement; maybe you just want to find people who understand what you've been through, or to build the kind of friendships that help you feel less alone, like the one Jarad and I discovered. That's where it begins. The same support networks that sustain advocacy also hold up the quieter revolutions, the ones that happen in homes, families and relationships. Because ending the cycle of violence doesn't just happen in parliament or on the news; it happens around kitchen tables, in text messages between friends and in the small, steady ways people learn to make their worlds safer. You just need *one* safe, steady connection. This is not a solo mission; it's something we do with others, not just for others.

Below are a few prompts to help you reflect on what your support system could look like – one that's built around trust, shared values and people who make you feel like yourself. There's no right way to begin. Just explore what feels possible.

1. **Begin somewhere safe – with yourself**
   Following on from our previous exercise, if speaking out feels too big right now (or always), start small.

Write your thoughts down. Record a voice memo. Say it in the mirror. You don't owe anyone your story, but you deserve to express it, gently and without judgment.

Start here: 'If I could tell the truth to just myself, it would be ...'

2. **Let people in, bit by bit**

   You don't need to overshare or explain everything. Just notice who feels trustworthy enough to hold a small piece of what you're carrying. Letting someone in doesn't mean giving away your whole story, it means offering a thread. See who holds it with care.

   Make a list: 'Who in my world has made me feel seen or understood, even in small ways?'

3. **Notice how they make you feel**

   Notice how your body feels around other people. Safe? Grounded? Respected? That's a clue. Explore this idea: 'After I speak with them, do I feel more like myself, or less?'

4. **Create intentional space**

   If it feels right, ask someone to catch up for a coffee, a walk or a phone call – not to trauma-dump, but to build trust. Let this be a space where you both show up as you are, not as who the world expects you to be. This all about creating an environment where connection can flourish.

Ponder this: 'Who's one person I'd like to spend more meaningful time with?'

5. **Explore shared purpose**

   You might not be ready to launch a campaign – and that's okay. But if there's someone who shares your values, your rage or your hopes, you can build something together. It might be a conversation. A support group. A creative project. Or just showing up for each other, consistently.

   Try this: 'Who might want to help create change, in whatever small way we can manage?'

You don't have to have it all figured out. You don't need a strategy, a platform or a plan for going viral. You just need somewhere to start and someone to reach out to who gets it, or wants to. Remember, movements begin with real people, not platforms – and so do the connections that change our lives.

The tasks you've completed here are a place to start, somewhere to explore what support could look like in your life, on your terms. Because once you find even one person who meets you in your truth, you're not alone anymore. And from that place, things start to shift. That's when change starts to feel possible.

Chapter 3

UNDERSTAND THE SYSTEM

If you've never been in a courtroom for a child sexual abuse case, let me paint the picture. Spoiler alert: it's nothing like the movies. There's no soaring orchestral music or lawyers passionately pacing the floor like they're auditioning for a TED Talk. No dramatic back-and-forths where a witness cracks under the pressure. No perfectly timed objections, no grand speeches, no gasping jurors, no final mic-drop moment that leaves the courtroom in stunned silence. You definitely don't get the satisfaction of watching Jack Nicholson in a shouting match with a young Tom Cruise, screaming, 'You can't handle the truth!'

What you get is something much colder. A lot of grey – grey walls, grey carpet, grey expressions. You get waiting. So much waiting. Long pauses. People speaking about you, not to you. You get benches that make your back ache within minutes, and enough legal jargon to make you feel like you've been magically transported into the middle of a university-level law exam that you never studied for. And right in the centre of all that sterile bureaucracy – often sitting quietly, surrounded by strangers in black robes and towering stacks of legal briefs – is a person who had the most intimate part of their humanity violated in the most cataclysmic way anyone can ever experience, who is now forced to watch the person who did it be defended.

And here's the kicker: after their abuser has been found guilty, and the survivor's truth has been heard, during sentencing, the judge will then read out testimonies as to what a great person the offender is; those defence-supplied character references I spoke about earlier.

I've never stood in court for my own case, but I've sat beside and supported survivors who have. Survivors who knew of the #YourReferenceAintRelevant campaign, who reached out to me via social media or email and asked me to come along. To sit beside them and bear witness. To hear the words they couldn't stomach hearing alone. It truly was one of the greatest honours of my life, and also one of the most heartbreaking things I've ever done.

It'll never not break my heart when I hear references written to defend and laud convicted child sex offenders. Like so many survivors, I see them in the news – tucked between legal gibberish and court summaries – and every time, it guts me. My chest tightens, my stomach drops and a familiar kind of ache settles in, one that feels like shame, rage, disbelief and grief all tangled together. A reminder of just how far we still have to go.

It doesn't matter how many cases I read, how many hearings I sit in or how 'prepared' I think I am – it is specifically those references that always cut so deeply for me. Because there it is, in black and white: a letter from someone who wasn't there.

Someone who didn't see the unbearable pain that child endured and hadn't heard the victim's voice tremble as they read out their impact statement. Someone who will never have to live with the flashbacks, the night terrors, the years lost to silence and survival.

And yet, they have the audacity to write, *He's a wonderful father.* Or, *He's a respected community member.* Or, *I've always known them to be kind, responsible and generous.* As if helping a neighbour move house or coaching the local footy team is somehow relevant. As if small acts of public decency cancel out years of calculated, private destruction.

It's more than just offensive; it's fucking dangerous. It tells survivors that their trauma can simply be outweighed by their abuser's reputation. That their truth is negotiable. That the person who harmed them simply holds more value in the eyes of the law.

This isn't some abstract idea for me. I've sat in those courtrooms. I've since found out about the glowing words my father's confidants wrote about him after he beat my mother to a pulp. I've seen survivors clutch tissues with shaking hands as those references were read out. I've watched them shrink into themselves, like they're disappearing, like every word chips away at their self-worth. I've seen firsthand the horror of watching a legal system bend itself to protect the comfort of the convicted. That pain stays with you, and it stains the memory of justice. It makes you wonder if the system ever really saw you at all.

That's the thing about the legal system. It's not just cold and formal – it's confusing, intentionally so. You need a barrister's thesaurus and a therapist on speed dial just to make sense of who's who in the room. There are the solicitors, the barristers, the judge, the registrar, the associate – and no one tells you what any of them do. The language is thick with legalese, the procedures move at a snail's pace, and you're expected to understand all of it while carrying the emotional weight of what happened to you.

For survivors, especially, the system can feel like a fortress with no front door. You don't get a manual for what happens when you decide to go to the police – how to find the words, how to relive the abuse without falling apart, or how to keep showing up when the process moves at the speed of paperwork. You're not handed a road map when you walk into a doctor's office, either. No one explains how clinical it can feel, how hard it is to talk about what's been done to your body while someone takes notes on a screen. You're expected to somehow know how it all works – the forms, the phone calls, the waiting rooms, the endless steps between 'reporting' and 'justice'. It's confusing, lonely and exhausting. And the worst part is that, half the time, it feels like the process is designed to protect the person who harmed you. And that's because it is. The system was built to protect the accused and to guard against state power, to ensure no one gets locked up without proof. And while that principle matters, that same system wasn't built with survivors in mind. It wasn't designed to hold the reality of trauma, to recognise grooming or to understand why someone might stay silent for years. It was designed to prioritise evidence over experience, procedure over truth and tradition over justice. And when it comes to sexual violence specifically, it fails us over and over again.

A 2024 report by the Bureau of Crime Statistics and Research found that, in New South Wales, only eight per cent of contemporary child sexual abuse cases reported to police result in a guilty conviction, and that's only among the cases that ever make it to the system at all. According to data from the Australian Bureau of Statistics, only one in five adult survivors ever report to police. So when you zoom out, the reality becomes stark: out of every one hundred reports made, a mere eight lead to any form of accountability. That statistic doesn't reflect a fair system at work. It reflects a system that fails the vast majority of survivors. A system where the burden of proof is so impossibly high, and the mechanics of trauma so poorly understood, that most cases never even make it to trial. A system where people who've already survived the unthinkable are forced to become legal experts, emotional contortionists and public witnesses to their own pain, just to be disbelieved anyway.

No wonder so many never come forward. When justice feels like another form of punishment, silence starts to look like self-protection.

I'll always remember the first time I sat in a courtroom and heard a character reference read aloud for a convicted child sex offender. It was around six months after launching the campaign. In November 2023, I attended the sentencing hearing for Paul Frost, a convicted child sex offender and former swim coach who groomed and abused eleven young students over more than a decade. He was found guilty of forty-three offences and sentenced to thirty-two years in prison, eligible for parole in twenty-four. Considering the sheer amount of abuse Frost perpetrated, that sentence might sound light and like a life sentence should have been imposed, but in the world of child sexual abuse prosecutions, it's practically a legal unicorn. Most offenders receive far less, which says a lot about the system.

Frost watched the hearing via video link from Shortland prison. He sat emotionless, sitting inside a cell, a grainy figure on a screen, while the courtroom filled with devastated parents, families and victim–survivors, each trying to find some measure of peace in the presence of a system that rarely delivers it. Judge Sarah Huggett delivered her remarks – how Frost had deliberately cultivated a culture of harm, normalised sexual talk with these children, encouraged inappropriate behaviour both with and between students, repeatedly offended in the school's changing rooms and storage areas, and other detailed accounts of abuse that are far too distressing to write in this book for you to read.

And then … she read the character references.

There were a few. One was from his mother, Lola Frost. Another, from restaurateur John Fink, creative director of the Fink Group, a prominent hospitality company founded by his father and behind Sydney restaurants such as Bennelong, Quay and Otto. Fink described Frost as 'hard working', 'devoted' and a 'champion and a protector of young people and children of all ages'.

Let that sit with you for a second.

This man had been found unequivocally guilty of forty-three separate charges of child sexual abuse. Yet respected individuals with reputations to protect stood up – not for the victims, not for justice – for him. They didn't speak to the irreparable damage he caused. They didn't acknowledge the survivors or the families whose lives had been completely shattered. They spoke instead about his character. To remind everyone just how 'good' he was. How 'polite'. How 'hard working'. As if any of that was enough to rewrite the truth. It was devastating. It was infuriating. And it once again confirmed everything I had felt: this system protects the wrong people.

After the hearing, I met with the parents of a survivor who had come to court in their child's place. When I introduced myself and told them about the campaign Jarad and I had launched, the tears came flooding. They thanked me and said they hoped it would succeed, that they wanted to see a day when no family would ever have to sit in a courtroom and hear the person who hurt their child be called 'a good man'.

It solidified why the work I do is worth every ounce of energy I've got.

I was speaking with one survivor of this case and, with their permission, I reached out to the media. I worked closely with Shannon Molloy, a journalist from news.com.au, to publish a detailed piece about the character references read in court.

When I walked out of the Downing Centre Local and District Courthouse in the heart of Sydney's CBD, there was a crowd of cameras, boom mics and journalists calling my name. The media circus had arrived but, for once, it was about something that actually mattered. Reporters crowded around to ask about the campaign, the good character references and why survivors deserve better. That day, the story was picked up by *The Guardian*, 7News, 9News, 2BG and a string of other outlets. This wasn't about chasing headlines or going viral, but about shining a light on the quiet, everyday injustices that unfold in courtrooms across the country – the kind that most Australians will never witness or even think about, but that haunt the lives of survivors forever. We were starting to shift the national conversation, and that mattered.

But if we're going to talk about how far we've come, we

have to rewind a little. Because understanding how we began to understand the system shows just how possible it is to change.

When Jarad and I first started the #YourReferenceAintRelevant campaign, we had no idea what we were doing. No media experience. No law degree. No political connections. Just two guys with an idea, lived experience, a shared sense of injustice and the wildly naive belief that maybe – just maybe – we could change something.

I had a rough idea of the legislation we had to change, but I didn't know who was responsible for criminal law reform. I barely understood how a petition worked. I had no idea where the fuck to start. And that's when I did what most people do when they have no idea what the hell they're doing: I reached out to someone way smarter than me.

Enter Michael Bradley, solicitor, writer, managing partner at Marque Lawyers and one of those rare people in law who doesn't just talk about justice – he actually lives it. Marque is a commercial law firm, sure, but they've got a serious human rights backbone, and Michael has long been known for his advocacy alongside survivors. I'd read his writing on *Crikey*, an independent media outlet – sharp, insightful and laced with real compassion. I'd quietly bookmarked him in my mind as one of the good ones, the kind of legal brain you dream about having in your corner if you ever wanted to engage in political reform.

It was actually one of my closest friends who gave me the push to reach out. We were talking about the campaign, and I was mid-spiral about what step to take next when they said, 'Why don't you just email Michael Bradley?'

Just. Email. Michael. Bradley.

As if I was casually DMing a mate to grab a coffee and not attempting to contact one of the country's most respected legal minds. But truthfully? I was so desperate. I didn't have a law degree, and I wasn't backed by a big organisation. I was just a twenty-three-year-old who'd had enough and wanted to make a difference in the world. So I figured, screw it. What's the worst that could happen?

So I did it.

I laid it all down: told him who I was, the idea Jarad and I had conceived – our mission to abolish good character references in child sexual abuse cases – and attached Section 21A(5A) of the *Crimes (Sentencing Procedure) Act 1999* (which, at that point, I had read more times than I'd like to admit). I admitted I wasn't legally trained, and I didn't try to overinflate myself or pretend I had all the answers. I didn't even ask to meet, just if he'd be willing to share a little insight.

Twenty-five minutes later, not only did he reply, he offered to meet in person.

Walking to the building and getting in the elevator, I was thinking, *Play it cool. Don't fidget too much. Don't accidentally swear within the first thirty seconds.*

When I walked into the meeting room, Michael was kind, warm and straight to the point. He didn't waste time, but he didn't rush me either. I explained the legislation. I told him the outcome we wanted to achieve. I walked him through the basic legal argument – or, at least, what I hoped was a legal argument. It was probably more of a passionate ramble peppered with phrases like 'this just feels wrong' and 'surely we can fix this?' But Michael didn't flinch. He let me speak, nodding thoughtfully, taking it in.

Then he replied, agreeing with my argument in general terms. But – and this is where things got a little more high-brow than my usual Google-level research – he said:

'It seems to me that whatever arguable utility character evidence could have in relation to sentencing, it couldn't be more than negligible. And it is clear that it often plays an outsize role in the thinking of sentencing judges. It's obviously counterintuitive to think about sexual offending in terms of exception – as in, "he's otherwise of good character".'

He paused, then added:

'It is nevertheless a difficult argument, because it goes against the general trend that favours rehabilitation. But I think the case is stronger in relation to child sexual abuse, because of the critical difference between that and sexual violence perpetrated on adults – the absence of consent as a factor of any relevance.'

Now, this language absolutely fried my brain. It was so much legal talk, I felt like I needed a translator, a week to think and three shots of espresso (and I don't even drink coffee). I just nodded along, like I totally understood, when really I was trying to remember whether 'arguable utility' was a compliment or a polite way of saying 'this is never going to happen'.

But then, after sitting with it for a moment, something clicked. Michael picked up the printed legislation I'd brought with me – Section 21A(5A) of the New South Wales *Crimes (Sentencing Procedure) Act 1999* – and read it carefully:

> (5A) In determining the appropriate sentence for a child sexual offence, the good character or lack of previous convictions of an offender is not to be taken into account as a mitigating factor if the court is satisfied that the factor concerned was of assistance to the offender in the commission of the offence.

He then looked up at me, pointed to the final clause and said:

'See this last sentence here …'

> … if the court is satisfied that the factor concerned was of assistance to the offender in the commission of the offence.

'This could be strengthened.'

He didn't mean strengthened as in making it harder for the court to decide; he meant the opposite, that we could make the law stronger, clearer, more survivor-focused by removing that final clause. That was it. Just one sentence needed to be taken out of the current law. One line. Twenty-one words.

But to me – to us – it was everything. Because tucked inside that single clause – that one dependent, conditional, lawyerly string of words – was the loophole; the reason so many convicted child sex offenders were still being described as 'upstanding citizens' during their sentencing. Unless the court could be completely satisfied that their so-called 'good character' actively helped them commit the crime, it could still be used to plead for a lighter sentence. It still left the door wide open for defence lawyers to submit good character references on behalf of their clients.

That sentence – vague, subjective, easy for a judge to dismiss – was the problem. And Michael had just confirmed it. What made this even more bizarre – and infuriating – was what Michael explained next: the law had already been partially amended in response to the recommendations from the final report of the Royal Commission into Institutional Responses to Child Sexual Abuse published in December 2017. That's why scout masters, religious leaders and school teachers couldn't rely on good character references in court anymore. The system had recognised that those roles enabled access to victims – and it rightly closed that door. But what about the perpetrators outside those institutional walls? What about Jarad's neighbour? What about my stepmother? What about the trusted family friends, the footy dads, the 'good blokes' who didn't wear a uniform or hold an official title, but still gained access through charm, deception and the soft power of social credibility? These were the predators hiding in plain sight, the ones who slipped through the cracks because they didn't belong to a church or a school, but still groomed entire communities into trusting them.

Michael Bradley didn't need to say, 'You're right.' He didn't need to draft a ten-page legal memo. Just four words: 'This could be strengthened.'

Michael didn't promise me the world. He didn't say, 'Let's get this to parliament tomorrow.' But he gave me something far more powerful: validation. Fuel to keep moving forward.

It was the first real confirmation that I wasn't delusional, that I wasn't making a mountain out of a molehill. That someone with legal knowledge and years of experience could see exactly what I saw: this could be challenged. It should be challenged, and that it needed to be changed.

The meeting only lasted about fifteen minutes, but when I walked out into the Sydney streets afterward, I felt like I'd been given a shot of adrenaline to the soul. That was the moment the campaign shifted into something legitimate. The rage I felt walking into that meeting was still there, but now, it had direction, a name and a legal target. And for the first time, I realised that maybe, just maybe, we were capable of going all the way.

And just when I thought I couldn't be more grateful, Michael did something extraordinary, something that turned our campaign from a compelling idea into a concrete reform proposal: he wrote the call to action for our petition himself. He just emailed it through to me a few days later. No fuss. No fanfare. It wasn't just supportive words – it was the actual legal draft, laying out the statutory amendment, the justification and the legislative language with clarity and conviction. The petition stated, in no uncertain terms, that sentences for perpetrators of child sexual abuse should not be mitigated by good character references. It highlighted the predatory nature of the crime – how grooming and manipulation are baked into the offence – and argued that so-called 'good' character is not separate from the harm but often a tool used to commit it. And crucially, it called for the deletion of just one line from Section 21A(5A) of the *Crimes (Sentencing Procedure) Act 1999*.

The next step – finding a political ally brave enough to take this on – would define the next stage of our campaign.

But before we get there in Chapter 5, I want to name something. Because even as I found extraordinary allies like Michael – people with legal knowledge and genuine integrity – I also began to understand why so many survivors have completely lost faith in the system. It's not just the confusing processes or the outdated language. It's the fact that the very institutions meant to uphold justice often feel controlled by a small, powerful group – what I've come to call the 'legal elite'. And they often seem far more at home in their wigs than in the realities of contemporary society.

The term 'legal elite' refers to a small yet influential group of lawyers, judges and senior legal professionals who occupy powerful positions within the justice system: think bar associations, law societies, legal commissions and advisory bodies. These people wield enormous control over courtrooms and have disproportionate influence over whether laws change – not because they're elected, but because they've embedded themselves in the structures that define how justice is interpreted and delivered. Instead of using that power to listen and adapt to the community – especially to the survivor community – they often cling to tradition and preserve the status quo. And in doing so, they create barriers to progress and hinder vital reforms for the most vulnerable within our community.

When Jarad and I launched this campaign in May 2023, we encountered resistance almost immediately. Not from the public – the public got it straight away – but from those on the inside. We were warned about 'unintended consequences' and the 'importance of individualised justice'. But when we pressed for real examples, they became vague and uncharacteristically inarticulate. They couldn't express what their actual problem with our proposal was. The only 'unintended consequence' that I – and plenty of legal experts who've escaped the ivory tower – could come up with was convicted child sex offenders serving longer sentences. And those consequences aren't unintended.

So why are we allowing a select group of individuals to be roadblocks to progress, to dictate the terms of justice at the expense of those most affected by their decisions? How can we justify preserving outdated practices that prioritise the interests of offenders over the safety of victim–survivors?

The truth is, not everyone resists this change because they think it's morally right – they resist because the system incentivises them to. For defence lawyers, character references are a strategic tool, a way to shave time off a sentence for a 'good bloke who made a mistake', even when that 'mistake' was the calculated grooming and abuse of a child.

When someone is convicted, sentencing is the last chance a lawyer has to influence the outcome, and good character references can shift the court's perception just enough to make a difference. A few letters and suddenly, the focus isn't on the crime. It's on the cricket coaching, the charity work, the clean record … everything but the abuse.

Recent polling backs this up. In July 2024, Resolve Strategic's founder Jim Reed published findings showing that just thirty per cent of Australians have confidence in our courts. *Thirty per cent.* That's a staggering statistic, one that reflects a growing disenchantment with a system that too often protects the powerful and abandons the vulnerable. In fact, when asked to describe judges, many respondents labelled them 'dumb smart people', a phrase that speaks volumes. It captures the public's frustration with a legal system that may be intellectually clever, but seems completely disconnected from lived experience and basic common sense.

And I see it play out every day in the comments under my posts – people wondering if justice is even possible anymore. People questioning whether the courts serve us, or just serve themselves.

It's hardly surprising, considering the constant stream of mistrials, crimes committed on parole, appeals, resignations, scandals, ludicrous sentences and inconsistent outcomes in various high-profile cases. Who could blame survivors and the broader public for giving up on the system altogether?

But here's the thing: we don't fix this by walking away. We fix it by dragging justice into the daylight and making noise, pushing for transparency, fairness and reform – not just from the outside, but from within. The erosion of public trust isn't just a political issue; it's a human one. Because when people stop believing in the justice system, they stop caring, and that apathy doesn't just stall reform – it threatens the foundation of our society. When people lose faith in the institutions meant to protect them, it breeds anger, disappointment, betrayal and a devastating sense of insignificance until, eventually, they disengage entirely.

That disengagement isn't abstract. It has real consequences. We've seen what happens when public trust crumbles: the rise of division, polarisation and blame. You only have to look at American politics to see how quickly disillusionment can spiral into chaos. Once people believe the system is rigged against them, they don't want to fix it – they want to burn it down.

Real conversation becomes almost impossible in that climate. We retreat into echo chambers, shouting and vilifying instead of speaking and listening. And while we're busy tearing each other down, the injustices we should be fighting together only deepen. That's how democracy fractures – not in one dramatic collapse, but in a slow, quiet erosion of trust.

So while the legal elite clutch their traditions and protect their procedures, survivors like Jarad and me – and the many, many others who've supported this campaign or launched their own – will keep showing up. We'll keep demanding change. Because justice should belong to all of us.

When I decided to pursue legislative change, I didn't have a law degree. I didn't speak in legal jargon or know how to navigate parliament. I didn't come from one of the traditional institutions that holds power in these spaces. I just had my story, my rage and a deep, unshakable conviction that something was deeply wrong, and someone had to do something about it.

It turned out it didn't matter that I wasn't a lawyer; what mattered was that I gave a shit, and I showed up, over and over again, with nothing but belief that we could build something better – and refusal to let the people in power look away.

And that, right there, is advocacy. Not just the kind reserved for those of us who want to campaign, but the kind that anyone can practise. It's when you stand up for someone who's being dismissed, when you challenge a harmful joke, when you refuse to stay silent in the face of cruelty. It starts with a gut feeling that something isn't right, and the courage to act on that feeling. It's about getting angry, and using that anger in a way that leads somewhere. That's what real advocacy looks like: showing up, wherever you are, in whatever way you can.

I still learn new things about the system all the time. I'm coming up on my fourth year of advocacy work, and I'm still unlearning, re-learning and trying to keep up. Because the system wasn't made to be easy – and it sure as hell wasn't made for people like you and me. It was designed to be complicated, impenetrable. To make us feel like we're totally insignificant. It was literally founded on the principal to protect powerful men and their 'property' – and that so-called property meant women and children. So of course it's hard. Of course it's confusing.

So, send that email. Make that call. Have that conversation. Be willing to fail. Overcome the fear that you'll fuck up … because, the truth is, you probably will. I have. Multiple times.

I've said the wrong thing, reached out to the wrong person, backed the wrong approach. But every single one of those moments taught me something. Every misstep helped sharpen and refine my vision for what this campaign could become. You don't need to get it right on day one. You just need to get started.

WHERE TO FROM HERE?

Advocacy, like survival itself, is about trial and error and persistence. It's about building a community of people who believe in the same change you do – whether they bring different skills, different experiences, even different perspectives.

Jarad and I didn't have the same story, but we had the same fire. We found each other, and that's where the momentum began. The most powerful thing you can do is find your people – even if it's just one person – and start chipping away.

This is a tough pill to swallow, but we're not going to dismantle this system overnight. I'd love nothing more than to build something better from the ground up but, right now, we must work within it. We push from the inside and wedge ourselves into the cracks and make space for others to come through. We change it bit by bit – one law, one policy, one conversation at a time. Maybe that doesn't sound revolutionary, or it sounds too slow. But let me tell you: the slow burn is still a burn. And change that lasts is change that's built with care.

Change doesn't begin and end with a viral Instagram post or a *Marie Claire* cover, but that doesn't mean they don't matter. They spark conversations, raise awareness and help to shape the broader culture. But real, lasting change is built in quieter, more personal spaces. In living rooms. In inboxes. In honest conversations over coffee with people who've lived through it. It happens when you take the time to reach out to someone in the sector and respectfully ask for five minutes of their insight. It happens when you refuse to give up, when you show up again and again, and say, 'I'm still here. I still care. I'm still trying. And I'm not going anywhere.'

MAPPING YOUR PLACE IN THE SYSTEM

By now, you've considered your story, your safety and your support network. You've taken some of the hardest first steps – naming the truth, reaching out and beginning to believe that maybe you could do something about it.

Now, it's time to start getting your campaign ideas down on paper. Think of this as a brainstorm, not a blueprint. This isn't about having a polished plan; it's about laying all the pieces in front of you and seeing what sticks. Don't worry if it's a dumpster fire of 'silly' ideas. Take your time. Use the prompts below as a jumping-off point. Circle what excites you and cross out what doesn't feel right. Add your own thoughts in the margins. There are no wrong answers here – just the beginning of something incredible.

1. **What system/s are you up against?**

   This could be a legal loophole, a workplace norm, a media narrative, a policy, a cultural script or even an algorithm. What's the structure or institution that allows this problem to persist? Who benefits from things staying the same?

2. **Who needs to care about this?**

   Not just politicians – think wider. Teachers. CEOs. Journalists. Voters. Board members. Parents. Funders. The aunties, uncles, cousins and grandparents making sure their young queer family members feel welcome at Christmas lunch. The friends who check in. The neighbours who listen. The people who model kindness when it counts. Who needs to understand what's really happening? Who could help shift the dial, even a little?

3. **Who's already working on this?**
   Chances are, someone's been fighting this fight before, and their work could help guide yours. Are there any organisations, journalists, existing campaigns or community groups already engaged in this space? Could you reach out, offer support or learn from what they've done?

4. **What's within reach?**
   Let's be real. You're probably not going to change a law tomorrow, but you might help stop a bad one from passing. You can push back when extremists try to wind back rights or control women's health. You can write a post, send an email, start a group chat, organise a lunch & learn, or reach out to someone you admire. Change doesn't always mean creating something new; sometimes it's protecting what's already been fought for. What's one small step you could take this week to build momentum?

5. **What makes your unique perspective powerful?**
   Your lived experience, your skills, your humour, your voice – these are not weaknesses. They're assets.

What do you bring that others can't? How could that shape your approach?

6. **What's your medium?**
   You don't have to be loud to be effective. What's your natural way of expressing yourself? Could you write about it? Talk about it? Paint it? Organise a spreadsheet? Start a meme account on Reddit? Tap into whatever your strengths are.

7. **What do you wish someone had told you sooner?**
   This can become the foundation of your message. Start there. What belief, truth or piece of advice do you want others to benefit from?

Get some paper, scribble down ideas, build a mind-map or jot down any names, concepts or to-dos that come to you. This is your working page. Come back to it whenever you feel stuck. Expand it as you go and let it grow with you.

Change isn't always loud. Sometimes it's scribbling an idea in your notebook on the train ride home. Sometimes it's the lump in your throat before you speak up in a meeting at work, or sitting in the back of a community hall meeting, wondering if you're out of your depth. Sometimes it's making eye contact with someone who says, 'I've felt that too.' Sometimes it's one brave person deciding they've had enough, and letting that be the initial spark of motivation. That's what real advocacy looks like. That's what moves the dial. And that's how you begin to understand – and eventually transform – the system. Change begins with someone who cares enough to try.

So no, you don't need to know everything before you begin. I didn't know what the fuck I was doing. I just knew I couldn't not do it. And neither can you.

Chapter 4

CRAFT A VISION WITH SPECIFICITY

Do you remember when Grace Tame became 2021 Australian of the Year?

I do, too.

I was staring at the TV with that wide-eyed, lump-in-the-throat feeling you only get a handful of times in your life – when something seismic is happening and you know, deep in your gut, that you'll never forget it. I could probably count those moments on one hand. The birth of my daughter. When I proposed to my fiancée. The imminent release of this book. And this moment, when Grace Tame was announced as the 2021 Australian of the Year. This wasn't just a woman standing on a stage making another speech. It was a moment of national reckoning.

There she was – powerful, composed, deliberate – standing centre stage on the most prominent platform in thc country and speaking not just as a survivor, but on behalf of other survivors who had been silenced for decades. There were no metaphors. No vague references to 'difficult journeys' or 'troubled pasts'. She said the words out loud:

'Child sexual abuse.'

And she did not flinch.

Grace spoke with a brutal honesty and spine-tingling clarity; a survivor telling the truth in front of the nation, refusing to look away. In doing so, she gave millions of people permission to stop looking away, too. I gripped the edge of the couch, breath caught in my throat, thinking, *This is different. This isn't just history being made. This is healing being televised.*

Then Grace finished her speech with a line that still gives me chills to this day:

'I remember him saying, "Don't tell anybody." I remember him saying, "Don't make a sound." Well, hear me now. Using my voice, amongst a growing chorus of voices that will not be silenced. Let's make some noise, Australia.'

That was not simply courage. It was revolution wrapped in a single, unflinching sentence.

I'd never seen anything like it. Until that point, conversations about child sexual abuse felt like they always happened behind closed doors – if they happened at all. It was a 'niche issue', or 'something that doesn't happen often', or a 'taboo topic' or something that was 'too heavy' for prime-time television. But here she was – an actual survivor, like me – being celebrated. Platformed. Listened to. Grace, a young girl who had been abused and silenced, reclaiming her voice on the nation's biggest stage, and inviting the rest of us to do the same.

It wasn't just that she spoke the truth – it was how she did it. Her presence was magnetic. Her words deliberate. She connected. She looked the nation dead in the eye and said, 'This happened. It's still happening. And we need to do something about it.' And beneath it all, you could feel the cost, the toll of being the face of a 'new' national conversation. The staggering weight of having to represent so many who had never been given the chance to speak. Of carrying all that pain and turning it into great purpose.

Grace didn't make it look effortless – you could see the tension in her body, the cost in her eyes – but she made *defiance* look effortless, like she was born to call bullshit. Like she couldn't unsee the truth, and wouldn't let anyone else pretend to either. Anyone who's lived it knows that kind of strength doesn't come cheap, and that kind of clarity doesn't just appear one day. It is earned, practised and fought for. It is shaped through pain and persistence.

After years of following her work from afar and drawing so much strength from it, I actually got to meet her. Grace Fucking Tame! My hero, standing right in front of me.

Now, I'm 6'3", so I did tower over her in stature, but spiritually? Emotionally? Existentially? I felt like an ant. I was trying not to sweat through my shirt. Trying not to stumble over my words, trying not to blurt out, 'You changed my life,' within the first thirty seconds. I think I lasted about seventeen.

I was so awkward. Think sweaty palms, heart hammering, fully rehearsed my 'hello' on the walk to the restaurant and still managed to fumble it. I didn't know where to put my hands. I had a brief internal crisis about whether I should go in for a handshake, a curtsy or just stand there like a wax figure from Madame Tussauds' Nervous-New-Activist collection. I think I ended up doing this weird hug thing.

Grace, being the effortlessly cool human she is, just gave me a warm smile and said, 'It's so lovely to finally meet you after talking on Instagram,' so casually, like she hadn't made national history a few years prior and singlehandedly ruptured Australia's silence around child sexual abuse.

Grace is kind. Real. Grounded. Fierce in the way only people who have been through hell can be. You expect someone like Grace to have a commanding presence – she's been on front pages, stood at Parliament House and detonated truth-bombs on live TV without breaking a sweat. In person, she wasn't intimidating. She was disarmingly warm, open and ridiculously funny. Like, actually funny – not 'Twitter funny', but proper Monty Python-type comedic genius level funny. Within five minutes, she had me laughing so hard, I forgot my own name. Which honestly, for a moment like that, was probably for the best.

We talked. I probably overshared. She didn't flinch. I remember thinking, *Well … this is fucking surreal.* She wasn't just a headline anymore; she was Grace. And somehow, despite everything she'd carried, she still had space for this tall, somewhat awkward, shy, sweaty-palmed survivor who was just trying to make sense of his purpose.

We stayed in touch, seeing each other through advocacy circles, events and mutual projects. Eventually, Grace very generously offered me a job at her foundation, and after two years of working behind a bar part-time to pay off the loans I took out to start my advocacy campaign (which, for the record, I do *not* recommend but will discuss more in Chapter 8), it felt like a godsend. For the first time, I could support myself while doing the work I actually cared about. The fact that the woman who I had watched on stage, who had cracked open the national conversation surrounding child sexual abuse, who I admired, was now trusting me to work alongside her? It was a pinch-me moment. It remains one of the proudest of my life.

I still have complete gratitude for the opportunities Grace has afforded me. Not just professionally, but personally. To be seen, trusted and backed by someone you admire so deeply changes you.

To this day, I consider her one of my closest friends. We don't talk every day – we don't have to – but when we see each other, we just pick up exactly where we left off. There's no ego or status games. No forced networking. Just two people who've crawled through the wreckage of trauma and decided to build something decent from the scraps. A deep, quiet knowing that comes from surviving the unspeakable, and choosing, still, to speak.

Watching Grace's journey up close – not just as a national figure, but as a person and a friend – has taught me so much. I've been able to see firsthand what values-driven activism really looks like. I've watched how she leads with integrity, how she speaks from lived experience without ever letting it completely define her and how she manages to bring unflinching clarity to some of the most complex, emotionally charged issues imaginable, all while keeping the heart of the matter front and centre.

There's a particular kind of wisdom that comes from walking through fire and then choosing to use that fire to light the path for others. Grace embodies that. She doesn't just speak truth to power – she speaks truth with purpose, not for the shock factor or to stir outrage, but to shift the dial and move us all forward.

I've seen how carefully she considers language. How she balances the weight of public expectation with her own humanity. Above all, I've seen how much it costs her to do what she does – the toll it takes to hold space for hundreds of thousands of other survivors while still trying to protect her own peace. It's no small thing to be a symbol, especially when all you ever wanted was to be a person. Grace carries both roles with extraordinary grace (pun very much intended).

If I had to distil everything I've learned from her into one lesson – one insight that has fundamentally shaped my own approach to activism – it's this:

Specificity is where genuine change begins.

It sounds almost counterintuitive at face value. When you're surrounded by so much injustice, narrowing your focus feels like letting things slide. Like you're ignoring the bigger picture or turning your back on the other twenty-five fires blazing in the house because you've chosen to focus on just one. However, if you want to change the system, you have to choose a point of entry, and if you start with clarity – with one clear, specific injustice – people can rally behind it. Legislators can legislate. Journalists can write about it. Survivors can feel seen in it. That's the power of focus.

And Grace's Harmony Campaign? It was a dead-set masterclass.

It was simple in its premise, but momentous in its impact: remove the word 'relationship' from legislation describing child sexual abuse. That the offence of 'persistent sexual abuse of a child' be worded exactly for what it is – abuse. Not romance.

Not a relationship. Not a mutual exchange or consensual interaction.

In 2021, Queensland, South Australia, the Australian Capital Territory and the Northern Territory still used legal phrases such as 'maintaining' or 'engaging in a sexual relationship with a child'. A *sexual relationship* with a *child*. It sounds inconceivable, right? Like something that surely got weeded out decades ago. But there it was, still embedded in the legal frameworks and courtrooms of multiple states and territories across the country. Slipping under the radar, cloaked in legal formality.

The problem with that kind of language is profound. It doesn't just describe the offence – it reshapes it. It softens the violence and implies agency, feeding into victim-blaming attitudes, easing the conscience of perpetrators and giving full licence for others to reframe grooming and coercion as 'romance'. As if a child is capable of consent. As if a power imbalance as immense as an adult perpetrator and child victim could ever be overcome.

For years, that one word – 'relationship' – sat quietly in legal texts around the country, distorting the narrative, and suggesting mutuality where there was none. Grace saw that. She named it. And then she went after it with surgical precision. She knew from the #LetHerSpeak campaign – the one that made her a household name – that a single, targeted reform could reshape the entire landscape. No noise for the sake of noise, no fifteen-point list of demands. Just one, very specific, deeply considered, razor-sharp call to action: *change that word.*

That's when it clicked for me. That's how change starts: with one word. One sentence. One clause that shouldn't be there.

One survivor who sees it and decides they won't look away. That's what Grace did, and in doing so, she showed the rest of us that you don't need to fix everything at once. You just need to start with something real, something focused. Something that matters.

That realisation completely reshaped how I approached my own campaign. Because when you're trying to change the world – or even just your local legal system – the temptation to scream about everything is very real. Every time you peel back a layer, you find another rot hiding underneath. Every time you learn something new, you're reminded of how fundamentally broken the whole machine is. It's overwhelming, and it makes you want to throw the entire structure in the bin and start again. And while I still fantasise about doing exactly that – taking the whole system, lighting it on fire and dancing around it like I'm Tom Hanks in *Cast Away*, screaming 'I have made fire!' – lasting reform requires strategy. It requires patience. It requires specificity.

When you're just starting out, when you're still learning the ropes and you don't yet have a seat at the table, screaming about everything can dilute your message. It confuses people and exhausts your audience. It makes it harder for the people in power (and the people you're trying to mobilise) to know what you actually want. But one clear, specific injustice? One problem you can name, and back up and speak to from personal experience? That's powerful. That's what cuts through.

You don't need a fifty-page blueprint for change. You need one clear target. A sentence you want rewritten, a loophole you want closed or a word you want removed. You don't need to be across every single policy document or legal precedent. You just need to care about something enough to say: 'That, right there. That shouldn't exist. And I'm going to do something about it.'

In my case, that 'something' was a loophole in the law that allowed convicted child sex offenders to be praised as 'good people' with character references during their sentencing. It sounds relatively small, doesn't it? One sentence. In one law. In one jurisdiction. It almost feels like an afterthought, the kind of change that might appear in the 'miscellaneous' section of a parliamentary report, nestled between authorising a plaque to honour a tree planted in 1983 and a motion to rename a highway after a retired politician. But what looks small on the page can cause a seismic ripple in the world beyond it.

Laws do more than just dictate rules; they signal what we value and they shape what we believe is acceptable. They define what we, as a society, choose to protect – and who we're willing to sacrifice in the process. When we change a law, we're not just amending words – we're altering the cultural script and redrawing the line of what is tolerated, what is overlooked and what is no longer up for negotiation. So yes, removing a single sentence might seem insignificant at first glance, but in reality, it's a direct hit to the old myths that have enabled abuse for decades.

The 'good bloke gone wrong' or the 'young man with a bright future ahead of him who just made a mistake'. The 'pillar of the community'. The myth that someone's reputation, standing or social capital is enough to excuse what they've done. When that clause is eventually gone and judges can no longer be persuaded to show leniency to a convicted child sex offender because their neighbour thinks they're a kind man who always helped to mow the lawn, something shifts.

It won't just shift inside a courtroom – it will shift outside of it, too.

Because the law doesn't always lead culture – more often, it follows it – but once it catches up, it cements what people have already begun to say out loud. The courtroom becomes the place where society's subconscious is made conscious. Where we hold up a mirror and declare, 'This matters. This no longer goes unchallenged.' Cultural change might spark the shift, but legal reform gives it backbone, and tells the next generation that this is no longer up for debate.

So, imagine this: no more newspaper headlines that paint rapists as 'troubled but talented'. No more glowing references from footy coaches or parish priests claiming that 'this behaviour was completely out of character'. No more soft-focus stories in the news that centre the offender's fall from grace rather than the survivor's lifelong climb back from trauma.

When we eventually close that loophole – when we say definitively, 'You don't get to be called good once you've caused this kind of harm' – we are doing more than changing sentencing practices. We are confronting the very stories that have allowed abuse to hide in plain sight for centuries.

The real magic of specificity is that it gives people an action they can take. It moves us out of the realm of vague outrage and into practical, purposeful reform. It gives people – especially survivors – something to do.

That doing part is critical. Outrage and pain are valid, but when you're stuck in the swirl of it – when your grief and anger have nowhere to go – it can eat you alive. Specificity gives the fire a direction, a point of entry. And for survivors who are often told that what happened to them is 'too complex' or 'too long ago' or 'legally insignificant', being able to act on one very clear issue can be life-altering. It says: *You don't need to swallow the whole world to be powerful. You just need to use your voice where it matters most.*

When Jarad and I first launched the #YourReference AintRelevant campaign, we didn't go to the public yelling, 'Fix the entire justice system!' We didn't list thirty ways the courts fail survivors, or the dozens of legal processes that needed reform. We went to them with one specific, gut-punching question: 'Why are convicted child sex offenders allowed to receive glowing personal references from friends and colleagues, read aloud in court, in an attempt to reduce their sentence?'

That was it; that was our ask. Not the moon or the sun. One clause, and a question. And because of that, people could wrap their heads around it. They could talk about it at the pub. They could share it with their friends. They could sign something. They could repost something. They could rally. Not just because they were angry (although many were), but because they knew exactly what to be angry about – and exactly what to ask for instead. And honestly, that's a real credit to Jarad and me (with Michael's assistance). We took a complex piece of legal rhetoric and translated it into a simple, human truth, one that anyone could understand, relate to and advocate for.

Because of that specificity, our work didn't just resonate with the public; it climbed the steps of parliament, landing in inboxes and briefings. It made its way into formal legal processes and caught the attention of governments. It reached briefing notes, ministerial inboxes and policy desks. And, eventually, it triggered formal action.

As I write this, two major reviews are underway that

directly stem from our campaigning. The first, in the Australian Capital Territory, is being led by the Justice and Community Safety Directorate. The second, in New South Wales, is being conducted by the Sentencing Council – the very body tasked with reviewing sentencing laws across the state. Both are examining whether good character references should continue to be permitted in the sentencing of convicted child sex offenders. These are real, full-scale, structural reviews of existing law, and they exist because of a single, specific ask that two survivors of child sexual abuse who refused to stay silent put forward, forcing the system to stop and take a second look.

What's even more telling is how the rest of the country has responded. Behind closed doors, state and territory Attorneys-General have told us the same thing again and again: 'We're waiting to see what happens in NSW and the ACT.' They're watching these reviews closely because they know the pressure is building, and the community is paying attention. And they know that once one jurisdiction moves, the rest will have to follow.

So yes, it started with one clause, but that clause is now the hinge on which national reform could turn.

WHERE TO FROM HERE?

Don't underestimate the power of narrowing your focus. Specificity is what transforms outrage into action. It's what carries your message from a conversation at the dinner table all the way into the legislative chamber. For us, that one sentence became the crack in the wall, the place where we started to apply pressure. And once the fault line is exposed, everything begins to shift.

So if you're reading this and feeling overwhelmed by the sheer volume of things you want to change – good. That means you care. That means you're paying attention. That means you've got fire. But now it's time to channel that fire and pick something and go all in. Not because the other things don't matter, but because this is how the work begins. This is how movements start. Not with a tidal wave, but with a ripple that refuses to be ignored.

REFINING YOUR FOCUS

By now, you've got a page (or six) of raw ideas from the last chapter – messy, sprawling and maybe even a little overwhelming. That's a good thing. You've mapped the landscape. Now it's time to zoom in. Remember, this doesn't just apply to campaigns or public reform. Change also happens on a micro level, inside families, friendships and homes. Maybe what needs reforming isn't a piece of legislation but a family culture built on conflict or silence. Maybe it's calling out name-calling, stopping a slur or setting a new standard for how people in your world speak to one another. Those small acts of courage are reforms too, just on a different scale. This is where you decide which hill you're going to stand on.

This isn't about dismissing the other issues – it's about starting somewhere, and starting strong.

Use these prompts to sift through your brainstorm and find your 'one thing':

Which idea feels most personal? The one you can't shake, even when you try?

Which idea feels winnable? Not easy, but possible with time, persistence and community?

Which idea lines up with your values? Think of the values you hold dear. Which idea connects most directly?

Which idea could be explained in one clear sentence? No jargon. No essays. Just the plain truth.

Which idea has the most potential to bring people with you? The one that is easy for others to understand, care about and repeat?

Now, put a star next to the one that ticks the most boxes. This doesn't mean you'll never work on the other. It just means *this* is where you begin.

The point of this exercise is to prove that you don't need to fix the world. You just need to find your thing, the issue that sits with you long after the news cycle moves on. The part of the system that makes you clench your jaw, and that you can't stop circling back to. That you talk about too much at parties. The thing that still burns when everyone else has gone quiet.

Because if there's one thing this work has taught me – one lesson that has been etched into my bones, reinforced by every win, every setback, every meeting, every media interview – it's that clarity doesn't just create momentum. It creates meaning. It gives people something to hold onto when everything else feels too big, too broken, too impossible to fix.

That's what Jarad and I have tried to do with the #YourReferenceAintRelevant campaign. It wasn't built on media headlines or handshakes in parliament – though, sure, those moments helped propel it forward. What gave it life, what made it land, was that anyone – regardless of age, education or lived experience – could hear what we were fighting for and say, 'Yeah. That makes sense.' It wasn't buried in jargon or hidden behind policy gates. It was human, a plain-spoken injustice that survivors could see themselves in – and that the public could grab hold of without hesitation, without needing a lawyer to translate it for them. It gave people language for something they'd always felt was wrong. And once people have the words, they don't stay quiet.

I think that's what Grace gifted all of us: the permission to do one thing at a time. To be unapologetically clear. Exact. To say the hard thing, with no euphemisms, and trust that truth will carry further than polish ever could. She gave us the blueprint. And she gave me, personally, the courage to follow it.

So if you're staring down a mountain of injustice and feeling paralysed by how much there is to fix, I'll say it again: you don't have to fix it all. You just have to start with that one thing, and then dig in. Be relentless. Be clear. Be explicit.

That's how you honour the people who've come before you. That's how you make space for those who will come next. That's how you build a movement that lasts, by whispering something true enough, focused enough that it becomes a roar.

We can all learn from Grace that clarity is its own kind of courage. And that one sentence, spoken boldly, can shift a nation.

That's what this chapter has been about. Not just the law or the loophole, but the lesson underneath it all: specificity is not a limitation – it's liberation. The clearer that answer, the more impact you'll have. You don't have to know everything; you just have to care enough to begin with one thing. And trust me, from there, you'll go further than you ever imagined.

Chapter 5

PERSISTENCE IS EVERYTHING

(BE PREPARED FOR REJECTION)

People love to romanticise persistence. They picture it like a training montage: inspirational music, tidy progress, triumph by sunset. Real life? No montage. It's a fucking grind. It's refreshing the same inbox like it owes you rent. It's rewriting the same sentence three different ways because you're pretending the adjective is the problem, not the system you're up against. It's silence that feels personal even when you know it isn't. It's walking out of a building designed to keep you out and wondering if the walls heard you at all.

Quick decoder so this chapter lands for anyone who's never dealt with parliament: you don't 'email the system'. You email peopl: backbench MPs, ministers, staffers who guard the calendar like it's the crown jewels. The attorney-general is the one who holds the pen on criminal law. To get an issue into parliament you usually need an MP to sponsor a petition or table it. Once a petition is tabled, the government has to respond on the record. That response can trigger a review (first by a department, then sometimes by an independent body). Reviews are slow by design – which protects us from knee-jerk laws – but it also means survivor-led reform can be dragged out for months or years unless you keep the pressure on.

Here's what persistence actually looked like for me inside that maze: I contacted fifty-one elected representatives in the New South Wales Parliament. Emails. Phone calls. Letters. Carefully worded subject lines so they stood out in inboxes. Lived experience in the body text. Links. Attachments. Follow-ups. A survivor asking the state to fix a specific harm.

I wasn't pacing the halls of parliament with a clipboard like a door-to-door salesman for justice. I was at my laptop, sending another careful email, hoping I'd finally found the combination of words that would land.

And, for the first fifty, nothing opened. Not a crack. Not even a, 'Thanks, but no.'

The fifty-first did.

THE FIRST FIFTY NO'S

Although I have my own political preferences, I didn't care who carried the petition. Labor, Liberal, Greens, even the bloody Nationals – this wasn't about party lines. It was about survivors. I just wanted Jarad's and my petition inside the building where decisions get made.

The responses, when they came, were the kind of polite nothing that sounds like progress if you read fast and don't think too hard. *We'll keep it in mind. Appreciate your advocacy. We recognise this is a complex issue.* Political white noise. The majority didn't respond at all. You can tell yourself not to take silence personally, but when your cause is your life, silence feels like a verdict.

There were nights I sat in front of the laptop with tears blurring the screen, wondering if I was kidding myself. I wasn't a billionaire or a lobbyist with a spreadsheet of donations and leverage; I was a survivor with a phone plan. Who the fuck was I to lobby politicians?

But then I'd think of thirteen-year-old me. The boy told to stay quiet. The boy who watched adults choose comfort over truth. He deserved a voice. All survivors do.

Somewhere, underneath the exhaustion, there was still a flicker of stubborn belief that one door would open. And one did. Abigail Boyd, a Greens MP in the NSW Legislative Council.

Abigail didn't skim. She didn't give me the 'sounds complicated' smile. She leaned in. She read the legislation. She listened. She saw past the jargon and understood the real-world harm: survivors sitting in court while their abuser's mates, coaches and colleagues stood up and told a judge what a good person the offender was. She clocked the legal, cultural and emotional impact. And she said yes.

That yes was oxygen, not because it solved everything, but because it made the fight real and gave us legitimacy. It took us from 'please listen' to 'you will be heard'.

Abigail agreed to sponsor our petition in the NSW Legislative Council. On paper, an e-petition looks like a webform. In reality, it's a crowbar. Once you gather the signatures (500 is the threshold in the council), the petition must be tabled and the government must issue a formal response. Translation: you can't be quietly ignored anymore. You force the system to look.

We launched. People signed. Survivors shared. The number ticked upward. I exhaled for the first time in months. It felt like we were nudging a door that was, finally, moving on its hinges.

THE PUNCH IN THE GUTS

Then the *Sydney Morning Herald* ran a piece. We'd pitched it to Perry Duffin, and he got it. The story spelled out the absurdity of the loophole and the momentum of the petition. It included a response from NSW Attorney-General Michael Daley: 'We have no plans to change it.'

A bland little sentence that hit like a sledgehammer from my own local member, a man I'd emailed, called, chased. The attorney for the whole state. The one person who could turn a petition into a reform.

I paced the living room, hands shaking, thinking about all the survivor stories I carried. How was I going to look them in the eye and say, 'Keep believing,' when the person with the power had basically said, 'Not worth it'?

From the next room, my grandma – who I was living with at the time – called out. 'Ray was talking about you today.'

'What?'

'This morning, on the radio. He mentioned the article. Your campaign. He sounded interested. Email him.'

A jolt of electricity. Ray was Ray *Hadley*, of 2GB, the conservative talkback behemoth. Not my usual lane, not my politics, but I wasn't naive about influence. Ray had the kind of platform politicians fear. If he was talking, tens of thousands were listening. And maybe – just maybe – one of them was the attorney-general.

I sat down and wrote the most important email of my life:

My name is Harrison, and I'm a survivor of child sexual abuse.

I laid out the loophole in plain language. I told him what it feels like to sit in a courtroom and hear your abuser praised. I told him about the petition and the attorney-general's brush-off. I ended like this:

If you have any platform for this issue, please use it. Not for me. For every child who ever had to sit through a hearing like that. It's not right. We have to fix this.

I edited that email three, four times. Tried to find the line between passionate and desperate, urgent and steady. Then I hit send. And waited.

A few hours later, my phone pinged. Ray had replied himself: *My producer will be in touch.*

The next morning, I was patched through live to *The Ray Hadley Morning Show* on 2GB. My hands shook as I held the phone. In the next room, Grandma was beaming. Her favourite program, her grandson on air.

Ray opened with the facts from the *SMH* story, then handed me the microphone. I walked listeners through what we were fighting for, explaining how Section 21A(5A) still allowed 'good character' references to be weighed at sentencing unless the offender's reputation had specifically assisted the offending, and how grotesque that is in practice. I could hear the shift in his voice as I spoke. He was moved. He was angry. And – crucially – he was backing us.

Ray ended by looking down the barrel of the biggest

microphone in the state and saying, essentially: *Attorney-general, meet with this young man. Hear him out. This law needs to change.*

That morning did what months of careful, polite persistence hadn't: it cracked something open. The petition exploded, with thousands of new signatures pouring in. And that night, my phone rang: an advisor from Michael Daley's office. After silence and a public dismissal, the attorney-general wanted to meet.

INSIDE THE ROOM

Walking into the Martin Place office that morning, I felt like every version of me showed up at once – the kid who kept a secret, the young man who hit post on a shaky Instagram video, the campaigner who had written more cold emails than I cared to count. Jarad was beside me, and we'd brought support from Full Stop Australia, a national organisation dedicated to combating sexual, domestic and family violence. The lift doors opened onto carpet that looked like it had never met a scuff mark. A receptionist smiled a steady government smile. Security passes clipped. Water in thick glasses. The choreography of power.

We were led into a boardroom with too much daylight and a table that could seat a cricket team. Minister for Prevention of Domestic Violence and Sexual Assault Jodie Harrison was there, senior advisors and the attorney-general himself. No small talk beyond the basics. No performative chumminess. It felt serious, which was all we'd ever wanted.

I didn't plead; I presented.

I laid out the harm in plain language: survivors sitting in

court, forced to hear their abuser praised as a 'good bloke' or a 'pillar of the community', while sentencing was being decided. I talked about the way those references rewrite reality in real time, how they blur the line between what a person once did well and what they have now been convicted of doing. I referenced the *SMH* story about Kshetiz Bhati, a convicted child sex offender whose sentence was reduced on appeal because the judge hadn't properly weighed his so-called 'good character'. It sounds absurd because it is, and yet under the law as written, it was entirely legal.

I acknowledged the usual objections before they arrived: yes, judicial discretion matters. Yes, unintended consequences deserve scrutiny. Then I asked the questions I couldn't get away from: why does preserving maximum discretion for a convicted offender matter more than preserving the basic dignity and safety of the survivor? Why is the system more afraid of limiting praise than of compounding harm?

To his credit, Michael Daley listened. Really listened. You could see him thinking it through in real time, trying to map what the next step might actually look like. What about offenders whose 'good character' was the very thing that gave them access to children (our point exactly)? How would this change fit with existing sentencing factors? What would we say to the bar association or law society?

I watched the shift happen as the understanding of our reform proposal started to land. The room softened, guarded faces turning curious, pens beginning to scribble into notebooks. When you've been knocking on doors for months, you can sense the moment one finally starts to open.

Nobody made promises – politicians almost never do in the

room – but before any petition was tabled, the attorney-general agreed to initiate a review through the NSW Department of Communities and Justice (DCJ). It's not the kind of thing that gets fireworks on the evening news, but for us, it was a tectonic shift. We had moved the government from 'no plans to change it' to 'we will examine it'. A door – finally – had opened.

I walked out into the corridor with Jarad and felt my whole body unclench. No fist-pump, or victory lap. Just a long exhale and a look that said, *We're in*.

The meeting didn't fix the law, but it did something I hadn't felt until that moment: it put our campaign inside the machinery. We weren't shouting through the window anymore. We were in the room, on the record, in the process.

THE VIEW FROM THE GALLERY

It wasn't just that one door. Abigail Boyd was still inside the building with a crowbar. When our petition was tabled, she stood and spoke to it. In that chamber, she became our voice. She told the council about Jarad and me, and the 4340 people who'd signed in the month it was live. (As I said earlier: the council only needs 500 to trigger a response.) She set out the basic common sense at the heart of our ask: a person convicted of sexually abusing a child cannot, by definition, be of good character. The law should reflect that truth.

From the public gallery, the room looked almost theatrical – polished timber, red leather, brass nameplates that have seen more governments than I've had birthdays. The clerks moved like clockwork. Papers up and down the table. Microphones clicking to life. It's funny what your brain notices when your heart is pounding. The smell of old books. The hush before a speech. The way one particular MP looked up when Abigail said 'convicted child sex offender', as if the phrase itself changed the air pressure.

Abigail's speech was surgical. No theatrics or fluff, anchored in numbers (4340 signatures in four weeks) and returning to the human truth at the centre: these references re-traumatise survivors and mislead the court about what 'goodness' even means. I watched heads tilt and pens pause.

When the petition was officially received and the next item moved on, I let out a breath I didn't realise I was holding. Jarad squeezed my shoulder. We didn't cry – though we could have. Instead we did what survivors do: we clocked the win and planned the next step. Submissions to draft. Meetings to request. Media to brief. We had shifted the question from 'Will anyone listen?' to 'What will the state now say for itself?'

That afternoon mattered. Seeing our petition formally tabled took the fight out of our laptops and into Hansard. 'Tabled' is a boring word for a very non-boring thing: the government is compelled to respond on the record. In our case, the attorney-general's response acknowledged the DCJ review already underway.

But the DCJ process revealed something we'd felt in our bones: total polarity. On one side, survivors, advocates and many in the community saying, 'This is basic.' On the other, elements of the legal establishment warning of apocalypse if a single mitigating factor is fenced off in these cases. The feedback was so split that, rather than let it calcify, the attorney-general initiated a second review, this time by the NSW Sentencing Council, the body specifically tasked with advising the government on sentencing law. Different chair. Different methodology. Different lens. Fresh oxygen.

That second referral told me two things: first, we'd forced the issue to a higher level of scrutiny, and second, the government understood it couldn't just file the controversy away. If DCJ was the first initial scan, the Sentencing Council was the specialist referral; the place you go when it's clear the issue runs deeper.

Here's why I'm labouring this moment: it proves that 'nothing is happening' is rarely true. Something is always happening – you just might not be in the right place to see it. A door opens. A meeting lands. A review starts. A petition is tabled. A response is forced. A second review is commissioned. Each piece looks small when you're exhausted and angry and you want the whole wall to fall tonight. But from the gallery that day, I understood what progress actually looks like inside a system built to move slowly; it's a series of required actions you've made unavoidable.

Since then, the review process has meant meetings, submissions, phone calls, clarifying emails and more waiting than I'd wish on anyone. And still – this is moving forward. Survivors deserve fireworks; they usually get minutes of meetings, but minutes add up. Reviews conclude. Recommendations land on ministerial desks. Drafting instructions go to parliamentary counsel and bills are born. Votes are counted. That's how the big yes eventually arrives.

So no, the law in NSW hasn't changed – yet – but the day we sat in that gallery, we forced the state to look at itself, and to keep looking. Once the machine starts speaking back, it can't pretend it didn't hear the question.

WHAT PERSISTENCE REALLY IS

If you asked me now to define persistence, I wouldn't say 'try, try again'. That's part of it, but it's not the heart. Persistence is adapting while you try again. It's learning what doesn't work and changing your angle without changing your aim. It's understanding that there are front doors, yes, but there are also side doors, service entrances, windows left unlatched, and, if you're willing to climb, chimneys.

Persistence is emailing an MP and getting silence, then writing to a radio host because your grandma heard your name on air, and trusting that allyship can come from places you didn't expect. Persistence is asking a Greens MP to sponsor your petition because the major parties are spooked this week and you don't have time to wait for their courage to grow. Persistence is bringing a peak body such as Full Stop Australia into the room with you because the system listens differently when a survivor doesn't show up alone.

It's also knowing when to rest, because collapse doesn't change anything. It's the private discipline of not curdling into bitterness after a public brush-off. It's getting up to do another interview, another meeting, another petition update when you'd rather disappear for a month. It's choosing the long game when a short, loud burst would feel more satisfying. It's not masochism or martyrdom; it's maintenance. You keep the engine running because you know you'll need it tomorrow.

WHY THIS MATTERS

People sometimes ask why I kept going when fifty doors stayed shut. Here's my answer: because the fifty-first isn't just a number. It's a reminder that the system may be slow, but it's not immovable. That an organised, specific ask can wedge itself into the gears. That one survivor's voice, multiplied by a community, can become a lever.

And because this clause – these twenty-one words – isn't some isolated annoyance. It's a symptom of an older myth we've all been taught to swallow: the 'good bloke gone wrong'. The idea that a person's reputation should soften what they did to a child. Every time a judge reads a glowing letter from a neighbour, a parish priest or a footy coach about a convicted offender's kindness, the message to survivors is clear: reputation matters more than your pain.

Removing that message from the courtroom matters. It won't heal everything or rebuild trust overnight, but it will stop one specific wound from being reopened, again and again, in the very place that claims to deliver justice. It tells the next survivor walking into that room that their truth won't be weighed against someone else's popularity.

THE DAY THE DAM CRACKS

Momentum rarely looks like momentum in the moment. It looks like admin. It looks like spreadsheets. It looks like staring at a loading screen that never seems to move. It looks like a politician replying, 'Can you come in on Tuesday?' and you saying, 'Any time works,' even though you're meant to be at your other job. It looks like a journalist asking follow-ups and you figuring out how to translate your fury into one line the public will remember.

Then, something shifts. You start hearing the same phrase in different mouths: 'We're watching what happens in NSW.' Briefing notes start to circulate. Terms of reference get drafted. The language you fought to make visible shows up in someone else's mouth. The attorney-general's initial 'no plans' becomes a departmental review; that review's polarity forces a Sentencing Council review. You can feel the centre of gravity move a few millimetres. Not a flood, but a crack, enough for new water to find a path.

That's persistence. Not just the knocking, the noticing and pivoting. The refusal to call a closed door a dead end, and the patience to let boring processes do their slow work, because you made it impossible for them not to.

TURN YOUR SPECIFIC ASK INTO A PERSISTENCE PLAN (YOUR 51ST-DOOR KIT)

You've got your specific ask from Chapter 4. Now is the time to build the stamina around it. You don't need perfect confidence to keep going – you need a plan for being ignored. Use this page as a working tool.

1. **Name your target (carry-over, but tighter).**

   What is the sentence/word/practice you want changed?

   ____

   Why? In one sentence a politician can repeat:

   ____

   ____

   If it changed tomorrow, the visible outcome would be:

   ____

2. **Build your first fifteen doors (diverse by design)**

   If your goal is public change, start mapping the network that can help you open doors. List fifteen people or offices across politics, media and civil society. Aim for variety:

   Three MPs (from different parties).

   Two senior advisors or chiefs of staff.

Two journalists (one mainstream, one niche).

Two peak bodies or non-government organisations.

Two community leaders.

Two legal minds (lawyer, judge or academic).

Two wildcards – people who might surprise you with their influence or insight.

If your advocacy is personal – if your mission is simply to end the cycle of harm within your own life – you can build your fifteen doors differently. Think of them as people who help you open healthier pathways. Make a list of local allies and potential allies.

They might include:

A close friend who really listens.

A family member who believes you.

A neighbour who looks out for you.

A teacher, manager or mentor you trust.

A peer support group or online community.

A counsellor, therapist or GP.

Someone who models the kind of calm and safety you want in your life.

Remember: you don't have to make a big, dramatic exit from relatives or friends who don't support you. You can quietly create distance – slowly, calmly and without guilt – while filling that space with people who bring genuine care, love and safety. Building your network, whether for activism or for healing, is about being intentional. It's about opening the right doors, not every door.

3. **Your one-sentence knock**

   Write the line that makes them care in twenty-five words or fewer.

   ____
   ____
   ____

4. **Your 150-word pitch (copy/paste backbone)**

   Draft a tight paragraph you can drop into emails, DMs or a media pitch.

   ____
   ____
   ____
   ____
   ____
   ____
   ____
   ____
   ____

5. **Follow-up ladder (dates you'll actually keep)**

   Day 1: Initial email/DM/phone message.

   Day 4: Polite follow-up + one fresh data point or story.

   Day 10: Second follow-up; offer a 15-minute call; include two times.

   Day 21: Final nudge; 'closing the loop' + attach one-pager.

   Day 30: Move to 'later' list; try a side door (different staffer/outlet).

Your calendar reminders

____

____

____

____

____

6. **Rejection reflection (use this space to write it out so it stings less and moves you forward)**

   Record it (date/outcome):

   ____

   The next person/office I'll try is:

   ____

   When I feel deflated, I will:

   ____

   One thing I learned from this 'no':

   ____

7. **Meeting agenda (make fifteen minutes matter)**

   Now, map out a tight fifteen-minute flow – opening, your exact ask, likely objections and clear next steps – and note the two outcomes you won't leave without.

   2 min: Lived-experience framing (why this matters)

   5 min: The ask (specific wording/scope)

   3 min: Address concerns (unintended consequences, discretion)

   3 min: Next steps (what I want them to do)

My two red-line outcomes for any meeting:

____

____

8. **Media micro-plan**

   Who's your 'unexpected ally with reach'? (Your Ray Hadley equivalent.)

   Three talking points (write them like headlines):

   ____

   ____

   ____

9. **Self-preservation boundaries (persistence ≠ self-erasure)**

   Max number of cold emails per week:

   ____

   A ritual after a hard 'no':

   ____

   ____

   A person I text when I want to quit:

   ____

   One thing I will not do to get a 'yes':

   ____

   ____

   Early warning signs I'm burning out:

   ____

   ____

10. What does persistence look like for me?

Today/this week, persistence looks like:

____

____

____

Why this fight still matters to me when it's quiet:

____

____

____

11. Your fifty-first door prize (be ready for the 'yes')

If someone says yes tomorrow, my next three actions are:

Step 1: __________________________________

Step 2: __________________________________

Step 3: __________________________________

WHY YOU NEED TO PLAN FOR THE NOS

You can't negotiate with silence; you can only outlast it. A rejection-ready plan turns the days that would normally make you spiral into days that quietly move you forward. It takes the emotion out of the logistics so you can save your energy for the rooms that matter. A plan means you pre-decide what happens after day 1, so you're not reinventing your courage every time someone ghosts you. It means you schedule follow-ups before you hit send; you keep a 'later' list so cold doors don't drain you. You write a two-line 'thanks anyway, keeping the door ajar' reply so a no becomes a breadcrumb, not a dead end. It means you cap your weekly outreach so your nervous system doesn't fry, and you build small rituals to close the laptop without carrying the fight into bed. Most of all, it means you treat each rejection as information: tighten the ask, try a new lane, move to the side door, come back with a bigger chorus.

SIX LESSONS I'M TAKING WITH ME (AND HANDING TO YOU)

Here's what I'm carrying forward from this chapter – the stuff I wish I had with from the start.

Don't accept silence. Keep knocking. The difference between failure and breakthrough is often one more unanswered email. If I'd stopped at fifty, I never would have met Abigail. I never would have sat across from the attorney-general.

Persistence is creativity. When the front door doesn't budge, try a side door. Or a window. Or go ask your grandma who she listens to on the radio.

Bring people with you. The system listens differently when you show up with community and with peak bodies. Full Stop Australia in that room mattered. Abigail in that chamber mattered. A big microphone at the right moment mattered.

Stay human. You'll be told you're too emotional, too naive, too impatient. Stay calm, but don't sand down your edges. Your humanity isn't a liability. It's the reason any of this matters.

Know which walls are load-bearing. Not every argument is winnable today. When you hit a fortified wall, that's useful information. Push elsewhere. Build pressure. Come back later with reinforcements.

Rest or you'll quit. You are not a machine for making meetings. Bake rest and boundaries into the plan. Step away when the noise starts eating your insides. (We'll cover this further in Chapter 8.)

CLOSING THE LOOP

People will tell you persistence is about having a thick skin. I don't buy that. I think persistence is about having a soft heart and a stubborn spine. It's caring enough to be hurt by the nos and still coming back with another ask.

If you want to push a system that wasn't built for you, you will be ignored until you can't be. You'll be told to wait for the 'right time', and you'll be discouraged by people who mean well and dismissed by people who don't. You'll meet gatekeepers, people who want to keep the fortress intact. And still you will keep going.

I can't promise your fifty-first door will open. I can promise this: if you build a plan that expects the nos and keeps moving anyway, you give yourself a chance to be in the right room when the yes comes. And when the yes comes, it won't just be yours. It'll be a signal to everyone still outside in the cold that the hinges do move and that persistence, however unglamorous, is still the most reliable tool we have.

At the end of the day, it's hard to beat someone who never gives up.

Chapter 6

USE SOCIAL MEDIA TO AMPLIFY YOUR MESSAGE

(WITHOUT LOSING YOURSELF)

Let me start with a confession that I think you will agree with: I don't believe social media will age well. Give it ten or fifteen years and I honestly believe a lot of people will step back – not necessarily because the platforms disappear, but because the constant noise becomes too heavy to carry. We don't yet have a clear long-term consensus, in peer-reviewed research, on how the always-on feed affects attention, sleep or stress, but it can't be good. And I don't need a study to tell me what my body already knows: when I'm plugged in too long, my chest tightens, my patience shrinks and I have the attention span of a goldfish. I forget what silence sounds like. I forget who I am when I'm not reacting.

And still, if you're trying to change anything in the current day, whether it's laws, workplace culture, environmental practices, school policies or a toxic norm in your friend group, social media is one of the most effective amplifiers you have. It's not the movement itself, but the megaphone that broadcasts it. Not the endgame, but a pressure tool that can pull a meeting forward, force a response, reach people who don't read press releases and turn something murky into something the public can actually see and understand. There's a real irony in the fact that a lot of activists – myself very much included – speak out against the world's billionaires while using the very platforms they own to do it. That's the moral paradox I live with now: use the tool, do not let the tool use you.

This chapter is about that balance. It's about how to post with a purpose that is authentic, targeted and human, and how to protect your mind while you do it. It's for survivors who want to turn pain into something that moves policy, or for those who just want to connect with others and feel a little less alone. It's for environmental campaigners who need to translate a 200-page report into one memorable line the public can repeat, for union organisers, community advocates, parents on a school council, anyone who has looked at a system and thought: *no more.* It's also a love letter to boundaries, because if your message wins but you lose yourself, that isn't a victory.

I'll tell you a story that proves how powerful a single post can be. Then I'll tell you what that power can cost, and how I stopped letting the algorithm decide who I was as a person.

WHY SOCIAL MEDIA IS A PHENOMENAL TOOL FOR CHANGE (AND WHY IT ISN'T)

This chapter is about getting your ask into circulation in a way that actually moves something. Think of social media as the top of a funnel: awareness → attention → pressure → meeting → process → reform. The internet is dynamite for those first three steps. But – and this is where a lot of well-meaning campaigns stall – likes aren't laws. Shares aren't safeguards, and views aren't victories. You're going to use the platform to push the door open, and then you're going to walk through it and do the boring, necessary work where the wins actually happen.

Social media can be one of the most powerful tools an advocate has, but only if you understand what it does well, and what it never will.

At its best, social media rewards clarity. If you can name the harm and the fix in one breath, it spreads. Online attention is built around simplicity. If your message lands cleanly and people can grasp it before they even finish scrolling, it travels fast. Timing matters, too. If there's a window of opportunity (usually while a story is breaking or public debate is heating up), you can reach thousands in hours instead of months.

That kind of speed has completely changed the way advocacy works. You don't have to wait for gatekeepers anymore; a single post can spark conversations that ripple far beyond your personal network. Before this, advocacy was slower and, arguably, heavier. It meant boots on the ground, not fingers on a screen. Back in the day, people organised in church halls and community centres, stuffed envelopes late at night, made calls from rotary phones and marched until their feet blistered.

(Well, at least that's what I've seen in films – I wasn't there; I was born in 2000.)

If you wanted to be heard, you had to show up in person. There was no instant feedback, no 'share' button, no dopamine hit of engagement. Just courage, patience and word of mouth.

Now, social media can give you instant scale. It lets you leap beyond your immediate circles and connect with people who didn't even know they cared. It invites strangers into movements they might never have found otherwise. And when enough people care, when enough people share, it creates pressure. Remember, the people in power – politicians, executives, editors – scroll the exact same feeds you do. They see the same posts, the same outrage, the same calls for action. And whether they admit it or not, when the noise grows, they can feel it.

Above all, social media runs on story. Data might convince the mind, but story moves the heart, and hearts are what shift culture. Humans move for humans. A face, a voice, an unpolished moment of truth – those things open doors that statistics alone can't. When you show your raw humanity, allow people to see themselves in you, you make it impossible for them to look away.

Still, for all its power, social media is not the place for everything. It's not where nuance lives, at least not at first. The feed is designed for skimming, not sitting with complexity. If you try to start with every layer of context, you'll lose people before they've even heard you. You have to lead simply and captivate attention with clarity, then guide people toward the deeper conversation elsewhere.

It's also important to remember that this work doesn't happen solely online. It happens in real-life interactions where people have to look each other in the eye and no one gives a fuck how many likes your last upload got. I've spent hours in rooms sitting with people who vehemently oppose everything I stand for and still had to find ways to keep the conversation going. I often hear people say things like 'Your campaign blew up because of social media', as if virality alone achieved change. I guess it's flattering, sure, but also reductive. The truth is, online and offline advocacy are different. They serve different purposes, reach different people and require different skills, but both matter. Young people with an idea are so often minimised and written off as 'influencers' as if that's their only form of power. There's always some cunt with a face like a cat's arse and an opinion, assuming they never leave their bedroom and just whinge online. It's such a lazy take. The reality is the online and offline worlds work in unison. My advocacy would be nowhere today if I hadn't shown up to protests, to functions, to meetings, to all the uncomfortable rooms that don't make it onto the feed.

And that's why it's crucial to understand that while the internet can witness you, it cannot hold you. It's not a substitute for care, or connection, and definitely not healing. The internet doesn't check in on you the next day to ask how you're feeling. It doesn't know what silence does to a person. That's something only the people around you can do.

It's also worth remembering that your self-worth cannot live in your reach. The likes, the shares, the comments, the views, the metrics can trick you into thinking your value is measurable. It isn't. You can go viral and still feel empty, and you can post something that reaches only fifty people and still change a life. Impact isn't always public.

Finally, once you share something online, you lose control of how it's received. You can't stop people from misunderstanding or twisting your words. All you can do is prepare for it, anticipate it and design your message to be as clear and misread-proof as possible. It's like an artist putting their work in the most prestigious gallery in the world: they can pour their heart into it, layer it with meaning and subliminal messaging, but there will still be some prick who walks in and says, 'My three-year-old could've done that.'

That's the contradiction of digital advocacy: you have to be simultaneously strategic and deeply human. Social media can amplify your message to the world, but it can't carry your whole heart. It's a megaphone, not a mirror. Hold those truths in your hands and you'll stop asking carousels to do a white paper's job, or your nervous system to be an emergency room. You'll make the internet serve the work, not swallow it.

ENTER: BONNIE BLUE AND ANNIE KNIGHT

If you weren't chronically online in late 2024, let me catch you up. Bonnie Blue is a porn star from the United Kingdom with a sizeable following on OnlyFans. Not exactly my cup of tea, but hey, each to their own. The issue wasn't her career choice. The issue was what she planned to do with it once she touched down in Australia. She publicly announced she was flying to the Gold Coast to film pornographic content for her subscription service – alongside Australian Annie Knight, who has dubbed herself Australia's most sexually active woman – with teenagers during Schoolies.

For those unfamiliar, Schoolies is a uniquely Australian

tradition: a week-long, post-graduation party for teens who've just finished high school. Think seventeen- and eighteen-year-olds drinking for the first time, kissing people they won't remember, dancing hard into the early hours, laughing about it in group chats the next day. It's a messy, awkward, formative celebration of youth and freedom. It's also a pressure cooker. Boundaries get blurry fast, and consent education matters more than ever. So when a porn star in her mid-twenties announces she's coming to film content with 'barely legal' teens, it's not just gross. It's hazardous.

What made the stomachs of myself, countless parents, survivors and Australians across the country churn wasn't just the content she planned to film – it was how openly, confidently and gleefully she planned to profit from it. This wasn't an offhand comment; this was a coordinated, public-facing campaign of sexual exploitation, dressed up as branding.

She used age and inexperience as the selling point, leaning on the language of youth like it was clickbait. She positioned herself as the sexually experienced adult who would 'take their virginities' and turn their most vulnerable moments into a monetised digital product. Her plan was crystal clear: glamorise it, promote it, profit off it.

The language used was deliberately predatory. Blue bragged, publicly, about having sex with 'fresh eighteen-year-olds'. She tagged her hotel and broadcast the filming location – Meriton Suites in Surfers Paradise – so Schoolies kids would know exactly where to find her. It was calculated, exploitative and wrapped in glossy internet culture.

What made it even more disturbing was the glaring power imbalance at play. Bonnie Blue, then twenty-five, is a financially powerful woman who knew exactly what she was doing. She wasn't luring in peers; she was targeting teenage boys – kids who'd just turned eighteen, still figuring out who they are, raised in a culture where mainstream porn is the blueprint and conquest is king. She didn't have to force them; she just had to make them feel chosen, and when someone with power makes you feel chosen, the question becomes whether that's ever truly free, informed consent at all.

Her plan relied on the larger toxic context of mainstream porn's influence on young men. From an early age, boys are exposed to content that tells them their value lies in conquest. Aggressive, dominance-based masculinity slides into their understanding of relationships, sex and self-worth. It's grooming – not by one person, but by culture. By eighteen, plenty of boys have internalised the idea that their worth is proven through the number of partners they can boast about.

This conditioning primes them for exploitation, and Bonnie Blue preyed on it. She knew those boys, impulsive, feeling invincible and steeped in the idea that any sexual advance is the ultimate social currency, would jump at the chance to be featured, proudly wearing it as a badge of honour.

Imagine being that boy. Eighteen. A porn star is in your DMs, calling you hot, telling you she wants to film with you. Your mates egging you on. Your phone blowing up. You're not thinking about power dynamics or digital permanence. You're thinking, *Holy shit, this is the coolest thing that's ever happened to me.* You don't realise your five impulsive minutes are about to be filmed, edited and uploaded into a machine that never forgets – clipped into compilations, embedded in search engines forever. You don't realise she'll make money off your naivety. That power you thought you had? You never really held it.

To understand why her plan was so insidious, you have to look at the larger context: mainstream porn's influence on young men. From an early age, boys are exposed to content that tells them their value lies in conquest. Aggressive, dominance-based masculinity slides into their understanding of relationships, sex, and self-worth. It's grooming committed not by a singular person, but by culture. By eighteen, plenty of boys have internalised the idea that their worth is proven through the number of sexual partners they can boast about. That conditioning primes them for exploitation. Bonnie Blue preyed on it. She knew those boys, steeped in the idea that any sexual advance is the ultimate social currency, would jump at the chance to be featured in her video proudly wearing it as a badge of honour, not realising the price.

I've heard a lot of people say, 'If a man did this to eighteen-year-old girls, everyone would be furious,' and sure that's true, but naming the difference should never be about defending men. Men overwhelmingly perpetrate the majority of sexual violence; that's not up for debate. Ask any woman in your life and she will have a story of harassment, coercion, assault, violence or fear she has carried in silence, and in most cases, no one batted an eyelid. There were no headlines, no viral fury, just another woman forced to move on. So holding Bonnie Blue accountable was never about flipping the narrative to, 'Oh, but imagine if a bloke did this' – that's not the point. It was about recognising that harm is harm regardless of who is causing it. It was about naming exploitation even when it doesn't fit the deeply binary cultural scripts we're used to. When the perpetrator is a woman and the victims are boys, society short-circuits. It doesn't know how to respond so it minimises, it sexualises, it laughs and it labels the boys 'lucky'.

Let me be clear: this was never about policing sex work, either. I don't do purity politics or pearl-clutching over OnlyFans. I'm not interested in shaming anyone who creates or consumes adult content. This was about predatory behaviour disguised as consensual content. About protecting young people – particularly boys – from being taken advantage of. About how exploitation can be marketed as empowerment when you strip away context and power dynamics.

Because Blue didn't just hint – she mapped it out. On TikTok, she posted a series of videos outlining her plan: fly to the Gold Coast, check into Meriton Suites with Knight, invite 'barely legal' boys to come find them. There was no effort at disguise, or any wink-wink. Just an open casting call for pornography, aimed at teenagers who had stepped into legal adulthood five minutes ago.

The comments started to split. Parents, survivors and advocates were horrified. Fans and plenty of men pushed back: *These boys are living the dream*; *You're just jealous*; *They're eighteen, it's legal – who cares?* That's when it clicked for me: if we didn't act, this wasn't just going to happen – it was going to be normalised.

So I did something simple and deliberate: I picked up the phone and called the hotel she'd tagged.

I filmed the call, a steady, thirty-second clip of me asking the front desk if they knew their premises were being advertised as a porn set. The staff member sounded blindsided; clearly, they weren't aware. I posted the video. No soundtrack. No edits. Just a clear, human question.

It blew up, with 1.6 million views, and 92,000 likes.

The comment section was on fire and my TikTok and Instagram tripled in engagement. Online petitions launched. The video ran on multiple news stations that night. Journalists messaged. Radio booked me. People tagged the Australian Federal Police, the hotel, the immigration minister. I was interviewed by news.com.au, *Mamamia*, SBS Australia, *The Daily Mail* and *The Briefing* podcast. In one surreal moment, I did a back-to-back radio segment where Annie Knight came on immediately after me to defend the plan. Bonnie Blue herself posted a response to my video:

> *You can't be phoning up and putting in a complaint about something that hasn't happened and implying that these men are underage and they're going to be intoxicated, which they're not.*

By then, the momentum was bigger than any one creator, and the story had shifted. It wasn't about a porn star flying in; it was about boundaries. It was about age. It was about the line between sex work and exploitation. It was about whether we're okay commercialising consent from teenagers who haven't even received their final year results.

The thing about politics is that when enough people are loud enough, fast enough, the system scrambles. Politicians may not care about your feelings, but they care about headlines, and this was a PR disaster waiting to happen. Within days – this part that still blows my mind – Immigration Minister Tony Burke cancelled Blue's visa. No press conference. No grand moral stand. Quiet, swift, decisive.

This didn't come from a multi-year lobbying campaign. It

didn't come from a national summit. It came from a fucking TikTok video – and from enough people watching and saying, 'This is not okay.'

Why did that post travel? Because it was specific: this hotel, this week, this plan. Because it was human: a real person making a real call. Because it gave people an off-ramp: clear targets to tag, clear asks to make. Because it drew a clean boundary: not anti-sex work; anti-predatory marketing to teenagers. Because it moved fast: inside the window where action could still matter. And crucially, it didn't stop at the post. The post was the match. The media, calls, meetings and escalation were the firewood.

That's what you need to understand. Social media isn't the movement, it's a tool. Used with specificity, clarity and urgency – contained, not allowed to consume you – it can tilt a decision in the real world. Used carelessly, it chews you up and trains you to mistake engagement for impact. The goal is not to feed the algorithm; the goal is to turn attention into pressure and pressure into change.

WHEN THE FEED BECOMES YOUR FACE (AND HOW I GOT MINE BACK)

Between the wins, there was a season where social media ate me alive. Not the cute 'oops I scroll too much' version. *Totally* consumed. I was on my phone before my feet hit the floor in the morning and long after the room went dark – refreshing, replying, deleting, posting, checking, repeating. I'd get headaches and close the app to breathe, but my thumb would reopen it before my mind remembered I'd decided not to.

Notifications weren't pings anymore; they were alarms. Each buzz lit up my chest like a house fire. I learned to read my value in analytics. If a post did numbers, I felt briefly worthy. If it flopped, I felt briefly worthless. I was a person with a pulse being graded by Instagram insights.

My DMs turned into an emergency room. Survivors poured their stories into that little box – raw, graphic, midnight-honest – and because I remember the exact feeling of finally being believed, I tried to hold them all. I answered strangers at 2.15am and ignored people I love across a dinner table. I postponed showers because of 'one more message'. I took the phone into the bathroom because 'one more voice note'. I told myself it was noble, and sometimes it was; often, though, it was compulsion wearing a cape.

That's the part I don't hear talked about enough: the way being a survivor can warp your work into penance. The voice that whispers, *If you stop, you're letting them win. If you rest, you're selfish. If you don't reply right now, they'll think you don't care.* I started confusing martyrdom for meaning. I convinced myself that exhaustion proved I was serious. I told myself I had to earn my right to be okay by bleeding a little online every day. The platform rewarded it. The algorithm trains you like a dog: here's a dopamine pellet for posting; here's some panic when you don't. Take a day off and your reach tanks. Take a week and you feel like you've evaporated. 'Consistency' is sold as discipline, but half the time it's fear that if you disappear, your cause disappears with you. That's a lie the machine tells, and I believed it.

Parasocial expectations crept in. People who did not know me felt entitled to all of me. *Any updates?*; *Can you share this now?*; *Why aren't you posting about (insert crisis here)?; You've gone quiet – what's wrong?* Some messages were loving, some were transactional, some were cruel. All demanded. And because I had built a space where survivors felt safe to land (which I am truly, deeply grateful for), I felt guilty for not being there at all hours with a soft landing and a perfect reply. I forgot I was a person and I became a feed.

My body eventually yanked the handbrake. Anxiety spiked. Sleep turned to wire. I woke at 3am with my heart in my ears, convinced I'd missed something important that only I could fix. My jaw ached from clenching. I rationed meals without even meaning to. The world shrank to a rectangle I couldn't stop looking at. I went back on antidepressants and anti-anxiety meds. I deleted Instagram off my phone for a stretch and felt phantom vibrations for days. I relearned quiet like it was a second language.

Then I did something painfully unsexy and life-saving: I built boundaries I could keep on my worst day, not just my best. App-free hours. Phone charging outside the bedroom. Lock-screen notifications off. A 'post and walk' rule for anything emotionally heavy – publish, close the app, go do something that involves my hands. I even wrote a copy-and-paste reply to messages for myself so guilt didn't have to improvise: *I see this. I'm grateful you trusted me. I can't counsel by DM, but here are three places that can hold you better than I can right now.* I scribbled a reminder in my notebook: *The internet is not therapy. I am not a 24/7 hotline.*

But this wasn't just an online problem. I realised how easily the same pattern can play out in real life too, especially when you've been the safe person for others in their pain. When people start to see you as their anchor, it can feel impossible to pull back, even when you're sinking yourself. Especially if those people have their own complex trauma. The guilt hits differently; that same little voice inside your head tells you that you're abandoning them, that you owe them constant care because you have the privilege of 'getting it'. But the truth is, empathy doesn't mean endless access. Being kind doesn't mean being available at all hours.

Finding balance is its own form of recovery. Sometimes that means responding slower. Sometimes it means saying, 'I love you, but I can't hold this right now.' You're still a good person if you don't pick up every time. You're still compassionate if you take a week to reply, or leave someone on read. You're allowed to protect your own nervous system before tending to someone else's. That's not selfish; it's actually you prioritising your own sustainability. Because if you burn out completely, you can't hold anyone, including yourself.

This section has hurt to write, because I am grateful – truly – for every person who found my page and felt safe enough to send a message. I don't take that trust lightly. But I had to accept a simple truth: I cannot be everyone's midnight, and when I try, I become no one's morning. I'm a better advocate when I remember I am not the algorithm's employee. I'm a better partner, friend and individual.

There's grief in stepping back from the online world. You lose the constant hum and the micro-highs. You lose the illusion that you're holding the whole thing together by staying online. There's relief, too. You remember what silence sounds like. You feel the sunlight on your face without calculating whether it's good enough lighting for your selfie. You watch a movie and it's just a good fucking movie. You eat with both hands. You answer the person across from you instead of the stranger inside your glowing rectangle. You have the energy to go to work and make a living. You start to feel excited to plan a holiday to somewhere you actually want to go, not where TikTok tells you to get a $22 hot chocolate. You start picturing a future that's yours, not one curated for or from the feed.

If you're going to use social media for your cause, build your off-switch into the plan the same way you build your talking points. Assume the post might work. Assume you might be flooded. Decide now, while you're calm, what Future You does when the inbox becomes an emergency room. Write the auto-reply, list the crisis lines, create the Resources highlight, identify a handful of moderators or peers who can take a shift when you need a day. Cap your weekly outreach so your nervous system doesn't fry. Give yourself a 'grief budget' for the week – three heavy threads you can hold with your full attention, then you stop. Schedule nothing for the hour after a big post. Walk. Cry. Touch a tree. Call someone who knows your real name. Remember you're allowed to say, 'I can't hold this today.'

I go deeper on burnout in Chapter 8, but I want to plant a flag here, for you and for me: surviving was not a job interview. You don't have to prove your worth by how much of yourself you spend online. You don't have to bleed to be believed. The kid you were does not need you to ruin yourself to make the world listen. They need you alive and present and able to laugh at something dumb on a Tuesday for no good reason.

I'm still learning this. Some weeks, I nail the balance; others, I trip and face plant into the comments. But I'm less interested in being endlessly available and more committed to being sustainably useful. And that shift – tiny, boring, radical – is the thing that keeps me here.

CHOOSE WHERE YOUR VOICE BELONGS

You don't have to be everywhere, you don't have to post daily and you definitely don't have to become a content factory to matter. Pick one or two platforms that suit your voice and your audience, then learn those rooms well enough to know where the light switch is in the dark.

If your strength is speaking plainly and looking people in the eye, short video platforms are your friend. TikTok (with Instagram Reels and YouTube shorts by extension) reward a human face saying one clear thing quickly. Think twenty to thirty seconds, subtitles on, and open strong: 'Here's the harm. Here's what needs to change. Here's what you can do.' These rooms are incredible for showing receipts – a recorded phone call to a venue, a quick walk-through outside an agency, a seven-sentence explainer you could deliver standing in line for coffee. The trade-off is nuance. You can't litigate every counterpoint in under a minute, and that's okay. Your job is to be precise, not exhaustive.

If you're a builder of tidy arguments, Instagram's carousels are your whiteboard. One slide, one idea. The cover slide says the problem and the fix in plain language. The last slide gives people an off-ramp: a link to email, a download, a submission portal, an RSVP. Stories are your rally space – little bursts to mobilise people with polls, link stickers, countdowns, and *we just hit 1000 emails, keep going* updates. I've noticed that the catch with Instagram (and it could just be my personal algorithm) is that it has moods that often mirror the news cycle. One week it's outrage, the next it's optimism, then suddenly it's back to collective despair. It's like the platform moves through emotional weather patterns, as we get swept up in them: so don't let the constant algorithm swing become a referendum on your worth. Just work your plan and ignore the noise.

If your audience includes journalists, staffers and policy people, treat X/Twitter like a newsroom, not a diary. Drop crisp threads with sources when news breaks, pin your ask and leave the brawls to those who enjoy them. When a thread lands, lift it into email and press, where it lives longer than a day.

If you need the neighbours – actual neighbours – Facebook is still the town square. Community groups, school P&Cs, local environmental pages, union branches: they live there. Frame your post like a noticeboard flyer: *Our park. Our river. Our school.* Then move people off-platform fast by collecting emails or RSVPs before the comments become a family meeting that lasts six days.

If your fight runs through boardrooms, LinkedIn can be surprisingly useful. Write like you're briefing a decision-maker: here's the risk, here's the fix, here's the business case. Don't just tag people, tag roles. Head of sustainability, general counsel, chair of the audit & risk committee, and so on. It sounds boring because it is. That's also why it works.

If you've got teachable depth, build a library on YouTube or a podcast so everything else can point there. The short stuff gets an audience's attention, while the long stuff earns their trust.

Let your ask choose your medium. If you need an urgent

ministerial response, a short video and a clear line on Instagram will set a room on fire fast. If you're pushing a corporate policy change, a tight LinkedIn brief plus a targeted press pitch will feel like knocking on a door. If you're educating over time, podcasts and YouTube are a garden.

HOW TO BUILD POSTS THAT ACTUALLY MOVE SOMETHING

People can't help but to share our feelings. We share things that stir us emotionally, something we can repeat easily because it makes sense in our mouths and in our guts. That doesn't mean simplifying your truth until it's flimsy; it just means shaping it so it can travel well.

Start with a single sentence that a stranger could repeat at a barbecue without checking notes. That one clear, undeniable question that makes people stop and think. 'Why does our council charge a fee to install solar panels?'; 'Why is the refinery allowed to dump into our river on weekends?'; 'Why can convicted child sex offenders be praised as "good blokes" at sentencing?' If the line doesn't roll off the tongue, you're not done refining.

Once you've found that anchor, build the post around it. Give it a spine and name the harm, name the fix, name the ask. Something like: *This clause lets a convicted offender be described as a 'good person' to soften their sentence. We must remove character references in these cases. Email the attorney-general, there's a template in my bio.* Those three things – the harm, the fix, the ask – are the foundation of any message that actually moves something. You'll be amazed how many arguments fall away when you make that structure clear.

Every good post also needs a human heartbeat. Data might convince people, but stories move them. If it's unsafe or inappropriate to centre someone else's story because of privacy, consent or risk, then use your own voice. 'I'm Harrison. Here's what I saw today. Here's what I'm asking.' The internet is full of polished logos and faceless campaigns; people stop for people, because we often see ourselves in each other.

It's also important to design your message for the way people actually scroll. Most are tired, distracted, holding cracked screens on the train to work or in bed at midnight. Hook them fast. Make sure your key line and your ask are visible before they even hit 'more'. Don't hide clarity behind aesthetics either. If the design of your post gets in the way of comprehension, strip it back.

Then think about where your audience should go next. Outrage without a verb is just rage bait and adrenaline. Give people a place to send that, whether it's a petition, an email, a hotline or a submission portal. Even a simple link that says, *Here's what to do next*, turns those emotions into action. That's how you build momentum.

If your post includes real people, protect them. Always get consent in writing, especially if trauma is involved. Offer anonymity, explain how far a post might travel – 'This could be seen by 100,000 people by tonight.' Give them an undo window and blur any detail that doesn't serve the point. You can tell the truth without replicating harm.

Finally, know when to log off. Decide in advance when to mute notifications, when to step back and let the post live without you. I usually give it twenty-four hours if it's hot, seventy-two if it's slow. After that, the comments and my brain are on separate leases. The work moves forward, and I move on, and you should too. You're not the internet's customer service line.

THE LADDER THAT ACTUALLY CHANGES THINGS

In my experience, most wins follow the same ladder. As I mentioned at the beginning of this chapter: awareness → attention → pressure → meeting → process → reform.

A good post sparks attention. Attention attracts journalists who need to file stories into a room that's already hot. Press gives you leverage for meetings: 'There's been a lot of public interest; can we have fifteen minutes of your time?' Meetings tee up process: petitions tabled, reviews initiated, inquiry terms set, submissions opened. Process can become reform: recommendations, drafting instructions, legislation, a vote. It's slow because it's meant to be; that slowness protects us from reactive laws. Your job is to keep tension on the rope without burning your hands.

When a post lands, your priority shifts immediately from 'managing comments' to 'converting momentum'. Email the right person with two or three crisp points and one clear ask. Keep it under 200 words and attach your one-pager: harm in one sentence, fix in one sentence, why now, who supports it, contact details. Bring a partner, and if a peak body, union or NGO sits beside you, doors become a whole lot more likely to open. Inside the room, ask for a procedural next step, not a vibe. 'Will you table this petition?'; 'Will you refer this to the Sentencing Council?'; 'Will you add this term to the review?' You are there to move the ball, not deliver a monologue.

ETHICS FOR A TRAUMA-INFORMED FEED

If you create a space where people bring their pain, you inherit a responsibility to them, and to yourself. That means having guardrails in place, even when you don't think you'll need them. Consent isn't a feeling; it's a structure. It lives in writing, in clarity, in systems that protect every single person involved. Get consent before you post anyone's story, even if their name isn't attached. Always offer anonymity where you can. Explain the reach and permanence of what you're about to share. If you're even slightly unsure, do not post. Waiting never hurts as much as regret.

When you share, make sure it's done with sensitivity and care. You can make your point without re-creating the wound. There's no need for graphic detail or identifying information, especially when survivors or minors are involved. That isn't censorship; it's compassion and empathy. It's knowing that you can still tell the truth without forcing anyone – including yourself – to relive it.

It's also crucial to signpost support. If you're talking about trauma, people will come to you carrying theirs. Keep crisis lines and specialist services saved in your notes so you can share them instantly. Perhaps having a Support highlight on your page for people to access might be a good idea? Remind others, kindly but clearly, that you're not a clinician and that your inbox isn't a triage area.

When people do engage, protect the space you've built. Freedom of speech does not mean freedom to harm; they're entirely different. You're under no obligation to host abuse or dehumanising comments. Delete what crosses the line. Block and report repeat offenders. You're not censoring anyone; you're curating a room people can breathe in. That's what safety looks like online.

Another line that's easy to cross without realising is giving oxygen to predators or bad-faith actors. You don't need to tag them or amplify their content. Now, I'm not saying refrain from speaking about the Donald Trumps and Andrew Tates of the world, but if someone online is being a pest, I recommend calling out the behaviour rather than the individuals. If you need to correct a lie, do it once, with receipts, pin it and move on. Your energy belongs to your cause, not in their theatre.

Setting expectations early saves everyone heartache later. A pinned note that says something like, *I read more than I can reply to. I'm not a crisis service. Here's who is* is an act of honesty. People can handle boundaries; what hurts them is confusion or silence.

It is integral that you take care of your nervous system like it's part of the campaign, because it is. Turn off notifications when you need to. Leave your phone outside the bedroom. Walk after posting something heavy. Eat something that isn't just coffee. Put your hands in something real whether it's cooking, gardening, Lego, clay, dirt, water – anything that reminds you you're still here, in a body, in a world bigger than your screen. It's easy to feel as though that is selfishness or self-indulgence, but that's just basic self-preservation and sustainability.

TROLLS, BRIGADING AND PILE-ONS

Before you post anything, take a breath and imagine the three worst comments you might receive. The bad-faith arguments, the deliberate misreads, the trolls who turn empathy into ammunition. Are you still comfortable posting what you planned? If yes, good. If not, adjust the frame. Strengthening your boundaries is crucial. Don't throw your nervous system into a pit.

If you do your job well, pushback will come. Some of it is honest disagreement, but plenty is just performative cruelty. You don't have to play with either. Before you post, write and pin your community guidelines – no slurs, no victim-blaming, no doxxing, no derailments. If you have the means, recruit one to three people you trust as moderators. Give them permission to delete and block without asking you to litigate every comment.

When the swarm arrives, remember: delete, block, move on. You will not persuade someone performing for an audience. If you receive threats, screenshot and report. Tell a real-life person. Don't carry it alone. And resist the urge to quote-tweet nonsense onto your main feed unless you're correcting a narrow factual claim for a clear reason. Don't feed the very fire you want to put out.

When someone misrepresents you, post a calm correction with receipts. Pin it, then go back to building. Let your body feel how boring that is. Boring is good. Boring is safe. If there's any chance a post wanders into defamation territory, get legal eyes on it. (I know, yawn.) The point is the win, not the catharsis of a spicy sentence that costs you three months' rent and a lawyer.

A NOTE ON IDENTITY AND THE CULT OF PRESENCE

There's a slippery slope between 'I need to be visible so my cause is visible' and 'I need to be visible so I feel real'. The same thing happens offline too. Once you start seeing yourself as the person who always says yes – the one who shows up, who supports, who listens – it becomes hard to ever say no, especially when the people reaching out are survivors: people whose pain you recognise in your own. But when you build your identity around being endlessly available, you start to disappear. You stop resting. You stop saying, 'I can't today'. You stop remembering that being helpful at the cost of your own health isn't kindness, it's erosion. Ask me how I know.

The guardrail I use now: does this post make the cause clearer and more actionable, or does it just make me louder? If I'm honest and the answer is the second one, I draft it in my Notes app instead and send it to my partner. Not everything you feel belongs in public, and not every thought needs a graphic.

Real advocacy also looks like speaking up in a meeting at work, emailing your kids' school with a clear ask, talking to your mate at the pub when they say something that needs pushing back on, showing up to a council consultation with three neighbours, or writing a submission that no one will 'like' on Instagram but that will sit on a desk when the decision gets made. A follower count isn't impact. Momentum off the screen is.

YOUR SOCIAL MEDIA STRATEGY

You've already did the specificity work in Chapter 4 and stress-tested it in Chapter 5. Now, use this page to turn that refined ask into a post-and-pressure plan you can actually live with.

1. **Your one-line thesis (20–25 words)**
   What's the sentence a stranger can repeat after one read?

   ____
   ____
   ____
   ____
   ____

   Name the harm (one sentence):

   ____
   ____
   ____

   Name the fix (one sentence):

   ____
   ____
   ____

   Name the ask (one sentence + link/action):

   ____
   ____
   ____

2. **Who is this post for? (tick two max)**

   ☐ Survivors

   ☐ Parents

   ☐ Decision-makers

   ☐ Journalists

   ☐ Local community

   ☐ Workers

   ☐ Students

   ☐ Other: ______________________________

3. **Platform(s)**

   Primary: ______________________________

   Secondary: ______________________________

4. **Format:**

   ☐ Thirty to forty-five second video

   ☐ Carousel (five to seven slides)

   ☐ Text + image

   ☐ Story sequence

   ☐ Thread

5. **Hook (first three seconds/first line):**

   ____

   ____

   ____

6. **Off-ramp (what can people do right now?)**

   ☐ Sign ______

   ☐ Email ______

   ☐ Call ______

- ☐ RSVP ______
- ☐ Donate ______

7. **Consent and care check (tick all that apply)**
   - ☐ Written consent for any story that isn't mine
   - ☐ No graphic details
   - ☐ Crisis resources included
   - ☐ Names/IDs removed if needed
   - ☐ Minor-safe
   - ☐ I am okay if bad-faith actors misread this

8. **Media escalation plan (if it pops)**

   Three talking points I can repeat anywhere:

   ____

   ____

   ____

   One person I can call to sanity-check live interviews:

   ____

9. **DM triage (copy/paste auto-reply)**

   Thanks for trusting me. I can't offer 1:1 support, but these services can: _________. If you're in danger, call ________. I'm rooting for you.

10. **Boundaries (pre-decide your limits)**

    Max minutes in comments today: ________________

    App-free hours: ___________ to ___________

Who I text when this gets heavy:

____

One thing I will not do for reach:

____

Early warning signs I'm burning out:

____

Reset ritual after posting:

____

Exit time (when I mute and move on):

____

11. Thirty-day content brainstorm.

Use the space below to jot down ideas for content you can post for the next thirty days. Here are some ideas for inspiration:

Week 1: Anchor ask + press pitch
Week 2: Proof + Nudge + Community highlight
Week 3: Human story + Q&A + Nudge
Week 4: Anchor follow-up + Partner spotlight + Event push

____

____

____

____

____

____

____

USE THE MACHINE, DON'T BECOME IT

Here's what I know now that I didn't know at the start: the internet will try to turn you into content. It will reward your most intense moments and punish your pauses. It will whisper that your worth is your reach and your reach is your worth. It will make you think that if you step away for a week, the cause will die and the world will forget you.

None of that is true.

You are allowed to be a person who advocates vigorously for what matters and still logs off. You are allowed to be someone who uses the algorithm like a borrowed megaphone and then puts it down. You are allowed to refuse to perform your pain for strangers as the price of being believed. You are allowed to recalibrate, to protect your sleep, to post less and do more, to move meetings forward quietly, to measure your impact by what changed, not by what trended.

Social media helped me crack open doors that should never have been closed. It helped me turn one specific harm into a public conversation, and then into formal action. It also nearly hollowed me out. What keeps me here now is a simple rule: I will use the tool; it will not use me. I will be loud when it serves the work and quiet when it saves my life. I will take the reach when it moves an agenda, and I will put the phone in a drawer when it doesn't. I will build the boring scaffolding that makes the spikes worth something – a petition tabled, a review commissioned, a clause rewritten. I will remember that likes aren't laws and shares aren't safety and virality isn't victory. I will stay human.

If you take one thing from this chapter, let it be this: post with purpose, guide people toward action or understanding, and expect the nos and silences without letting them define you as a human being. Whether you're leading a cause or just sharing your own story in a personal capacity, your truth always deserves protection. Build your boundaries into the work so you can still recognise your face in the mirror. And when you get that thirty seconds of clarity or a moment that cuts through the noise and makes the system move, take the win and keep going.

Posts fade, but movements don't. So make the post, then make the call, schedule the meeting and advocate for the change. And in the spaces between those things, be a person who laughs with their friends, goes for a walk without a phone, books a weekend away to relax. Because that, too, is part of the work.

Chapter 7

SPEAK, EVEN WHEN YOUR VOICE SHAKES

Have you ever seen *Batman & Robin*?

Not *The Dark Knight*, the masterpiece with Heath Ledger redefining the Joker. Not Robert Pattinson brooding his way through *The Batman* reboot either. No, I'm talking about the gloriously chaotic 1997 disaster starring George Clooney as Batman, Arnold Schwarzenegger as Mr Freeze, and a plot so baffling it somehow decided the most logical fuel source for Arnie's freeze gun was diamonds.

It was a campy, bizarre fever dream with acting so wooden, you could've built a house with it. The costumes (featuring the infamous bat nipples) looked like rejected Eurovision entries. And yet, despite its eleven per cent rating on Rotten Tomatoes – and the fact Clooney himself apologised publicly to fans for its existence – I absolutely love it.

Maybe it's because it's so outrageously bad it loops back around to being weirdly brilliant. Or maybe it's because, somewhere between the blacklight neon fight scenes and Mr Freeze unironically shouting 'Chill!' as he freezes a room full of innocent civilians into popsicles, there's actually a scene that hits a little too close to home.

Clooney's Bruce Wayne is standing by the fireplace after an argument with his sidekick, Robin, and asks his servant, Alfred Pennyworth, 'Am I pig-headed? Is it … is it always my way or the highway?'

And Alfred, ever the wise old butler, answers, 'Why yes, actually. Death and chance stole your parents. But rather than become a victim, you have done everything in your power to control the fates. For what is Batman if not an effort to master the chaos that sweeps our world? An attempt to control death itself.'

Bruce looks away. 'But I can't, can I?'

And Alfred simply says, 'None of us can.'

It was around midnight, camping with my fiancée in the south of France. We were crashed on the fold-out bed in our campervan, tipsy with French riesling and a dinner I'd cooked crouched like a human pretzel, watching on my laptop – when, of all things, this scene from *Batman & Robin* hit me harder than it had any right to.

Because that's what living with trauma can feel like: a constant, exhausting attempt to control a world that refuses to be controlled. An endless push for comfort, predictability and safety, even if that safety is an illusion.

For years, I stayed in the same suburb where I was sexually abused. I built my life around familiarity, even when familiarity meant fear. After trauma, the unknown isn't exciting – it's fucking terrifying. I avoided all risk. I wasn't really living so much as surviving inside a bubble of comfort, with an addiction to McDonald's meals, six Coca-Colas every day and social anxiety keeping me anchored in place. I still battle that pull today. Some days, I dream about jumping on a plane to Vietnam and starting fresh where no one knows my name. Other days, the weight of conditioning presses so hard on my chest that even the idea of catching a train into the city feels impossible. That's the pendulum of complex trauma: swinging between the craving for escape and the gravitational pull of crippling fear.

This is why campaigning isn't necessarily the answer for everyone. Healing doesn't always mean turning your pain into a cause. Sometimes, purpose looks quieter, like building a life that feels safe, loving the people who show up for you or learning to exist without the constant hum of survival. Maybe it's in the way you raise your kids differently to how you were, or how you speak to yourself when you're struggling. All of that is important; all of that counts.

Campaigning – and especially using the media to influence change – felt, and sometimes still feels, like being thrown into the wild with nothing but a torch and a very nervous laugh. Because if there's one thing you can count on with the media, it's that you can't control it. You can't script it, you can't predict it and you definitely can't bubble-wrap yourself against it. If you choose to advocate in this way, you have to step into the chaos, the unpredictability and the discomfort and get loud anyway.

For those survivors who choose to live more privately, the same truth applies, just in a different way. You can't control how people respond to your story, or whether they understand it, or if they ever do. You can only control how you hold it. How gently, how firmly, how much you let it define you. Whether you speak out publicly or choose privacy as self-protection, both require immense courage. Both are acts of strength in a world that often demands pain be performed.

If there's one thing survivors like me crave, it's predictability. After living through child sexual abuse, I developed a kind of sixth sense for scanning my surroundings and planning everything down to the minute. It's like my brain decided that if I could script every scene of my life in advance, nothing could ever blindside me again. Unpredictability was the enemy; it meant danger could be lurking around any corner.

But as I learned that night in the campervan with my partner (and countless other times throughout my life), unpredictability is everywhere. You can't keep life hermetically sealed in a Ziploc bag. Tents leak, possums invade and sometimes your own emotions ambush you like a rogue comic-book henchman. The fear of not knowing what might happen next had been holding me back more than I realised. It wasn't just about surprise realisations from a campy action movie, it was about the bigger mission I was on. I was so afraid of things going off-script in my activism that I almost didn't step up at all. What if an interviewer blindsided me with a question I hadn't rehearsed? What if a politician reacted with anger instead of support? What if my voice cracked right when it mattered most? All those worries swirled in my mind and nearly convinced me that staying silent was safer.

But here's the irony. Doing nothing felt safe – and it was slowly eating me alive. I had a cause that meant the world to me and a story that I knew could help others, but only if I shared it. Sharing it meant stepping directly into the unpredictable spotlight I had been avoiding. It was like wanting to be Batman, yet being terrified of leaving the Batcave (okay, enough *Batman* references now).

The epiphany I felt during the scene nudged me forward. If a silly old movie could catch me off guard and make me feel something powerful, maybe unpredictability wasn't all bad. Maybe it was a sign that I was alive, and that I cared deeply. Maybe the quivering in my stomach was not a signal to hit the brakes, but the rumble of an engine starting up. I began to see that discomfort could be a catalyst. The unpredictability I dreaded could become the source of my power, if I leaned into it instead of running away.

So I made a deal with myself: I would start saying yes to things that scared me in that special way – the way that meant I was onto something important. My hands might shake and my heart might do the cha-cha, but I'd do it anyway. In other words, I'd use my discomfort as fuel instead of as a cage, and find a way to be okay with not being okay.

The first time I truly tested this new philosophy was when I was invited to share my story at an annual general meeting for Full Stop Australia – a national organisation dedicated to combating sexual, domestic and family violence. I was supposed to give a short speech about my story and why Jarad's and my campaign mattered. Old me would have spent a month writing and rewriting a perfectly polished script, memorising statistics until I dreamt in pie charts, and practising in front of the mirror so many times that my reflection needed a vacation. New me – well, new-ish me – decided to wing it with just a rough outline and a whole lot of brutal honesty.

When the day came, I stood in front of a small crowd filled with very important people, palms sweaty, feeling my voice tremble as I started: 'Hi, I'm Harrison James and I'm really nervous right now.' Great opening line, I know, but it was the truth, and at least it got a chuckle and some sympathetic nods. So I kept going, heart thudding. Instead of spouting every data point I had crammed in my brain, I spoke about why I cared so much. I talked about the moment my life changed, about the faces of people we were fighting for (including my own in the mirror). And yes, I even admitted how scared I was to be speaking out – but that my fear was exactly why I needed to do it.

A funny thing happened: the more candid I was about being unsure and vulnerable, the more the audience seemed to lean in and listen. I saw wet eyes and clenched jaws. My voice did crack (so much for that worry – it happened and the world did not end). In fact, that crack might have been what cracked them open. Afterward, people came up to hug me. I got over my awkwardness with hugs pretty quick that day. They thanked me for 'telling it like it is' and 'saying what they felt but didn't know how to express'. My raw honesty had lit a spark.

I walked out of that meeting feeling two feet taller – which for me, at 6'3", meant I was basically brushing the ceiling with my ego. I hadn't delivered a slick speech and I had no idea if I stayed within the time limit, and I might have even dropped a few f-bombs during it (oops). But none of that mattered, because the message got through. My authenticity was more convincing than any pie chart or perfectly crafted soundbite. It turns out people have a finely tuned BS-detector and a deep appreciation for genuine vulnerability. In a world of spin, being real is radical.

That day, I learned that my story – in all its messy, emotional glory – was my superpower. I didn't need to pretend to be the flawless hero. In fact, the flaws and cracks were where the light shone through. Raw honesty became my rocket fuel for inspiring change. Every time I owned up to the fear or pain or hope I was carrying, it reminded me why I was doing this in the first place and recharged my drive to keep going.

Emboldened by the positive response at the AGM, I knew I had to keep pushing myself further out of my comfort zone. And that's when one of the biggest tests yet landed in my lap: *Sky News*.

Now, for anyone unfamiliar, *Sky News Australia* isn't exactly the place you go if you're hoping for warm hugs and moral support. It's a network infamous for platforming commentators who have consistently hurt, minimised and dismissed the survivor community, including people like me. To say I fucking despise the outlet would be putting it lightly.

So when a *Sky News* producer invited me on for a live interview, everything in my body screamed, *Are you kidding? Absolutely not.* I knew what they stood for. I knew how survivors like me had been treated by voices on that very platform. The easy choice – the comfortable choice – would have been to politely decline and stay in safer spaces where I knew I'd be met with compassion and understanding.

But comfort doesn't change the world. And as much as I hated the thought of sitting at that news desk, I knew it was an opportunity to hold them accountable on their own turf.

So I said yes.

On the evening of the interview, my nerves were in overdrive. In the studio, under the harsh glare of cameras and countdown clocks, I could feel the tension humming through me. Jaynie

Seal, the host, sat across the desk, smiling professionally. The crew counted down. *Three … two … one …*

We were live.

Jaynie opened. 'Child sexual abuse survivor and co-founder of the Your Reference Ain't Relevant campaign Harrison James has given an update on the progress made in New South Wales in reviewing the use of good character references in child sexual abuse cases. Harrison is joining me live now – thanks so much for joining us. Tell us a bit about the campaign you set up.'

I smiled, took a breath, and said, 'Sure – and before we dive into the discussions regarding the Your Reference Ain't Relevant campaign I run, I just wanted to acknowledge that *Sky News* has been home to countless individuals – both presenters and regular guests – who have consistently dismissed and hurt my community, the survivor community. And as a survivor, I know fellow survivors watch my work very, very closely. The last thing I ever want them to feel is disappointed in me for sitting at this desk. But I also recognise that as an activist who speaks out in this space, I can't just have conversations in echo chambers where I feel safe. Sometimes you have to step out of your comfort zone and have difficult conversations in places where you won't necessarily be agreed with – because child sexual abuse is far more pervasive than most people want to realise, and it's going to take efforts from absolutely everyone to tackle it. So that's why I'm here: to have these discussions.'

Live. On air. I called out *Sky News* on *Sky News*!

Jaynie was visibly taken aback – blinking hard for a moment – but the interview continued. We shifted into discussing the campaign, the legal reforms we were pushing for, and the survivor-led movement gaining momentum across Australia. I kept my composure, speaking from the heart, steady even as my hands trembled slightly under the desk. I knew every word mattered.

When the cameras finally cut, Jaynie turned to me and asked, half-awkward, half-curious, if I had an issue with a particular presenter or staff member.

I simply said, 'No. I just spoke truth to power.'

Then I stood up, walked across the eerily silent newsroom – past two employees who stared at me like they'd just witnessed a ghost walk through their set – and out into the cool air.

My hands were still shaking, my stomach still knotted. But my heart? My heart was steady.

Because I had done exactly what I set out to do: speak, even when my voice shook. Step into discomfort. Hold my ground. And show survivors – and myself – that you can stand in the lion's den and still refuse to lose your humanity.

For those who will never stand in front of a camera, the same lesson still applies. Your lion's den might be a family dinner where someone says something cruel. Speaking up doesn't always mean doing it publicly; sometimes it's finding the strength to say, 'Hey, that's not okay,' even when your voice trembles. It's standing in small, ordinary rooms and choosing to stay kind, stay calm and stay firm in what you know is right. That, too, is bravery. That, too, is how change begins.

That day taught me something profound: the media is not a mirror. It's not there to validate your worth or reflect your soul back to you with kindness. It's just a tool, a megaphone you can use – even when it's cracked, even when it's held by hands you don't trust – to carry your message further than you ever could shouting alone.

Would I ever willingly watch *Sky News*? No fucking way. Would I ever pretend the network hasn't caused harm? Also no. But in that moment, sitting at that desk, I remembered that the real audience wasn't just Jaynie Seal; it wasn't just the camera crew or even the handful of people scrolling *Sky News* at home. It was the survivors out there who needed to know that someone like them could walk into an uncomfortable, hostile space and still speak their truth with dignity and strength.

That host probably forgot about me five minutes after I left, but someone watching might remember what I said for five years. And that someone might be a minister weighing up reforms, a journalist deciding what story to tell next, a survivor gathering the courage to speak, a parent grappling with what justice really means, or even someone locked inside their biases – someone whose knee-jerk reaction has always been to doubt, dismiss or blame victims – nudged a few millimetres toward empathy.

Once I wrapped my head around media as a tool, not a mirror, it freed me. I didn't need to obsess over looking foolish or being liked. I reminded myself that I'm not doing this to get gold stars for presentation; I'm doing this to ignite change.

Activism demands that you sometimes get uncomfortable. Speak even when your voice shakes. Find your power in the places you'd least expect it.

Now, let's talk about the megaphone itself – the media platforms, especially the old-school ones. We know they're not perfect. Legacy media (think big TV networks, newspapers) can be sensationalist, reductive and sometimes downright hostile to people trying to challenge the status quo. They'll cut your quotes down to the juiciest five seconds, slap on a headline you didn't ask for and occasionally pit you against a professional troll in a panel discussion.

After that *Sky News* spot, a part of me wanted to swear off mainstream media forever and retreat to the comfort of writing long posts for people who already 'got it'. But then I remembered something a mentor once told me: you don't win change by only preaching to the converted. I had to reach people beyond my bubble, and many of the people beyond my bubble still got their info from legacy media – even the frustrating channels and papers that often got it wrong or oversimplified.

So, I made a strategic decision: I would engage with these flawed megaphones, but strictly on my own terms.

That meant first choosing my opportunities wisely. Not every media request was worth my time or sanity. I learned to do my homework before agreeing to anything, researching the show, the outlet, the host. If it was a place known for little more than shouting matches or manufactured outrage, I often passed. But if it had a sizeable audience – especially one that included the kinds of people we needed to reach and sway – I'd consider it, even if it wasn't exactly a friendly environment. Sometimes the rooms that are hardest to walk into are the ones that most need to hear you.

It also meant sticking relentlessly to my message once I was in the door. Interviews are like rivers; they can meander wildly if you let them. Legacy media loves tangents, soundbites and drama. I wasn't there for fireworks – I was there to solve a problem. So whenever a question started drifting into useless territory, I would gently, almost stubbornly, steer the conversation back to the core message. It felt a little like being the designated driver after a wild party: everyone else might want to veer off course and pop through the drive-through, but someone had to stay focused and get the car home.

Crucially, it meant refusing to take the bait. There were moments when a journalist or a panel opponent – often the type who loved to play devil's advocate with a pose of faux-intellectualism, treating conversations about abuse like thought experiments rather than something that affect people's lives forever – would try to drag me into a personal attack or an irrelevant debate that had nothing to do with the discussion at hand. And believe me, every ounce of my being wanted to bite back and call them a massive cunt, but I learned to channel the energy of a second grade primary school teacher: calm, firm, no-nonsense. I'd say, often with a polite smile, 'That's not why I'm here; I'm here to talk about how we prevent the sexual abuse of children in Australia.' I'd say it over and over again if needed, like a broken record that refused to play their tune. 'Kill them with kindness' is my motto, some would say to a fault.

I learned to use every media hit to our campaign's advantage, even the ones that didn't feel like victories. If an article twisted my words or framed our campaign as 'controversial' (deep breath, deep sigh), it still served a purpose. We'd grab the coverage, share it with our supporters, highlight the parts that mattered and ignore the spin. Because at the end of the day, the fact remained: our issue was being talked about on prime time and in national papers – places where decision-makers and voters were watching. Visibility, even imperfect, helped validate that our campaign wasn't just a niche grievance – it was a national conversation that demanded action.

Engaging with legacy media was like trying to ride a somewhat rabid horse: you hold on gently but firmly, guide it as best you can and accept that it might try to buck you a few times. But if you manage to stay on, you can cover a lot of ground you otherwise wouldn't. Flawed or not, those outlets gave our campaign visibility far beyond our own echo chamber, and the bottom line was that I couldn't afford to ignore any megaphone handed to me, even a dented, screechy one. Our cause was just too important.

The media hustle wasn't about chasing attention – if it had been, I would've found an easier, far less emotionally taxing path. There are simpler ways to get noticed, like reviewing bottled water brands on YouTube or filming prank videos at shopping centres. But it wasn't the point. Every time I spoke up publicly, it was about creating visibility for the cause, so moments that mattered could happen.

One of those moments found me sitting in a small but polished office in Canberra, across from Senator David Pocock (a personal hero of mine). Not long before, he'd been captaining the Wallabies rugby team; now he was tackling legislation. And here he was, genuinely listening to me – not checking his watch, not half scrolling through emails. Fully present.

I hadn't got there through any insider connection or political grooming. I was there because enough noise had been made that it became impossible for decision-makers to keep ignoring us. The media attention – the articles, the interviews, the growing public pressure – cracked open doors that otherwise might have stayed closed. Jarad and I had flown to Canberra with nothing but a folder of letters from survivors and supporters, heads swirling with nerves, stomachs doing gymnastics. There was a part of me that worried I wouldn't seem polished enough, or that my lack of a law degree or public policy training would be obvious the second I opened my mouth.

But the meeting wasn't about our credentials. Jarad and I shared what brought us there: our lived experience, our campaign's goals and why this issue wasn't just important but urgent. I didn't deliver a rehearsed speech. I spoke plainly, outlining what it's like to live with the impact of broken systems and what small changes could mean for real people. At times, my voice wavered. Emotion caught in my throat when I spoke about some of the worst days survivors like me face, or about losing my daughter. I fumbled for words once or twice and the sky didn't fall in. No one ushered me out of the room. I noticed again that the more honest I was, the more I let my natural nerves and emotions show, the more seriously I was taken.

David didn't need a policy wonk that day. He needed to hear from someone who had lived through the aftermath of injustice. Someone who could connect policy proposals to actual human cost. It reminded me, once again, that authenticity isn't a weakness. It's the sharpest tool you have in rooms built to intimidate you. Vulnerability, not polish, was what shifted the energy. Walking out of that meeting, I could feel it in my bones that something had shifted, not just in the conversation, but in me. I hadn't been perfectly composed or armed with a hundred statistics. I had come as myself – anxious, heart-on-sleeve, determined – and that had been enough.

But I knew one meeting wouldn't change the system. This issue was bigger than one office, one party or one state. It needed a groundswell of understanding across political lines, and I needed to be willing to keep walking into rooms that scared me.

A week later, I found myself on a Zoom call with Senator Fatima Payman, a young, trailblazing politician who brought her own lived experience into every conversation. Speaking with her felt less like a formal meeting and more like connecting with someone who understood what it meant to feel out of place and push through anyway.

We swapped stories about learning on the job, about figuring out the rules while already playing the game. There was no performance in that call, just a mutual understanding that advocacy and politics alike are built by people who dare to keep showing up.

Then came a meeting with Zali Steggall, a former Olympian who defeated former prime minister Tony Abbott (insert eye roll here) to win her seat in parliament. Sitting across from someone who had built her political career on sheer determination and courage was both humbling and galvanising. She emphasised the importance of building unlikely coalitions – finding ways to connect with people who didn't necessarily see the world the same way I did, but who could still be moved to care. Those words stayed with me. Advocacy isn't about preaching to the choir. It's about reaching people who might not yet understand, and giving them a reason to care.

Each meeting and conversation reinforced the same lesson: I didn't need to posture or perform. I didn't need to pretend to be an expert in areas where I wasn't. I needed to stay rooted in what I knew – in the truth of lived experience, in the urgency of the cause, and in the unpolished, sometimes shaky way that truth spills out when you care deeply. It turned out that the very things I once thought disqualified me – the shaking voice, the messy emotions, the impostor syndrome – were the things that connected me to people in power.

Speaking when your voice shakes doesn't make you weaker.

It makes you undeniable. It reminds people sitting across from you that the policies they shape aren't just abstract frameworks; they are lifelines for real human beings.

The lesson was simple but powerful: you don't have to erase your humanity to be heard. You just have to be willing to show up as you are, again and again, even when everything inside you says it would be easier to stay quiet.

One of my biggest fears, whenever I entered a meeting or interview, was the dreaded question I couldn't answer. What if they asked about subsection 5.3 of some law, or a statistic from a report I missed? What if they used an acronym I didn't know?

Early on, I almost let this fear paralyse me. I felt I had to read every report, know every figure by heart and anticipate every curveball. Basically, I felt I needed a PhD in Everything Ever to justify speaking on my own life experiences. This is both impossible and unnecessary – a double-whammy of wasted energy. I learned a beautiful truth: you don't need to know everything to make a difference. Politicians have researchers and advisors for the nitty-gritty. What they needed from me was the human angle, the story, the why-it-matters-in-real-life testimony that all their briefings and spreadsheets couldn't provide.

If I got a question I didn't know, I learned to say, 'I'm not sure about that, but I can get back to you,' or 'That's a great point. What I do know is …' and then connect it back to lived experience. Not once did someone sneer, 'How dare you not know the GDP of 1972!' They understood I was there as a citizen advocate, not a walking encyclopedia.

Showing that I didn't know everything sometimes even helped. It gave the person across from me a chance to fill in the blank, to contribute to the conversation, making it more of a collaboration. When a senator asked, 'Have you considered how this might play out with the existing XYZ program?' I admitted, 'I haven't, to be honest.' That opened the door for them to explain it to me, and then we brainstormed how to address that angle. It became a team effort instead of a pop quiz.

So if you're ever holding back from speaking up because you think, *I'm not expert enough*, please toss that thought in the bin. Your experience is expertise, and your passion and perspective are enough. You can always learn facts and figures as you go (or google them later, like the rest of us), but no one else can bring your voice to the table. I didn't know everything – I still don't – but that hasn't stopped me, and it sure as hell shouldn't stop you.

Remember that *Sky News* interview? It was a surreal moment, but the truth is, it wasn't just that one interview that got people to pay attention. It was the cumulative weight of every media appearance, every press release, every radio interview, every article, every spot on the six o'clock news, every time we refused to let the story fade into silence.

I can't even count the number of media releases I sent out. Every time we had an update, a new petition milestone, a meeting scheduled with an attorney-general, a survivor willing to share their story, I pushed it out to journalists, local papers, national outlets, whoever would listen. Sometimes it landed, sometimes it didn't. I kept going. That persistence across platforms built a momentum you could feel. Slowly, the inbox began filling with messages: survivors reaching out to say thank you, journalists wanting quotes for articles, politicians' offices requesting meetings or asking for briefings.

It shouldn't have to be that way. It shouldn't take standing under the harsh lights of television cameras or trending on Instagram to be heard. But that's the reality of campaigning in a crowded, distracted world. Visibility forces acknowledgement, and it made our cause something even the busiest lawmakers couldn't easily ignore anymore. Before the media attention, we were easy to dismiss: just another group of activists. But once our message was echoing across newsrooms and comment sections, we became harder to sideline. Jarad and I weren't just a couple of passionate individuals anymore; we were a movement being watched. That growing visibility opened doors I never imagined would open. It led to meetings not just with empathetic independents such as David Pocock, Fatima Payman and Zali Steggall, but with members of every major party, across every shade of the political spectrum.

There were plenty of meetings with old-school MPs from the major parties, too – the kind of politicians who probably thought the only good kind of activist was one they didn't have to meet. I was warned more than once to expect dismissiveness and, sometimes, that's exactly what I got. A few opened meetings by commenting that they had seen 'my little TV interview', in tones that ranged from polite interest to thinly veiled scepticism.

I never walked into those rooms unprepared. I made it my job to understand who I was speaking to. Some MPs cared deeply about public safety. Others were focused on community trust. Some were drawn to arguments about economic efficiency or political optics. So instead of leaning solely on moral grounds – even though the moral case was clear – I tailored the conversation to meet them where they were. I framed our reform as a way to make communities safer, courts more trusted and processes more consistent with public expectations.

It worked. Not always instantly, and not always completely, but often enough to keep hope alive. I saw the atmosphere in the room shift – from arms folded and guarded expressions to curiosity to requests for more data, follow-up briefings or offers to 'raise it with a colleague'. It didn't happen because I morphed into someone I wasn't. It happened because I stayed true to the message while being strategic about how it was delivered.

Building cross-party support was like assembling a coalition of unlikely allies. Everyone had their own motivations, but the outcome was the same: momentum for reform. Was it exhausting? Absolutely. There were days I felt like I lived out of parliament houses across states, and nights where I drafted emails until my brain short-circuited. I even had dreams where I was stuck explaining the campaign to a crowd that kept multiplying, like some weird activist stress dream. But every meeting was a chance to turn discomfort into action. Every conversation was a step closer to real change.

Looking back, it's clear that every breakthrough moment in this journey was born from a moment of discomfort. Every time I thought, *I can't do this, it's too much*, and did it anyway, something good came of it. Not perfect, not immediately world-changing, but good, incremental and empowering. From getting emotional over *Batman & Robin* in a campervan I could barely stretch out in, to stumbling my way through a speech with shaking hands at an AGM, to sitting under the harsh studio lights facing a sceptical TV host, to walking into daunting ministerial offices where the stakes felt sky-high,

I kept choosing the path that scared me. I chose discomfort over retreat, and that made all the difference.

The big secret I've learned is that courage feels awful before it feels awesome.

We tend to imagine heroes as confident, unflappable figures who charge into battle without blinking. In reality, courage often starts as terror – or, at the very least, an incredibly uneasy feeling in your gut. It's your knees knocking as you stand up to speak at a town hall meeting. It's your hand shaking as you send that email asking for help, knowing you might be ignored. It's your voice quivering during a live television interview. It's the lump in your throat as you walk into a minister's office to tell them something they might not want to hear. It's telling someone you love, 'There's something important I need to share with you.' It's raising your hand in a work meeting when your heart is hammering against your ribs. It's clicking *publish* on a post about something you've stayed silent about for years. It's walking into a protest alone because you know it matters. It's asking a question in a classroom full of people who seem smarter than you. It's showing up to your first therapy session and admitting out loud: 'I need help.'

It's discomfort. Plain and simple.

But if you can push through that flaming ring of discomfort – if you can keep going even when everything in your body is screaming for you to retreat – you come out the other side stronger, braver and more powerful than you ever knew you could be. Courage doesn't feel good at first, but it builds something in you that lasts far longer than fear ever could.

And here's something practical that helped me do it again and again: scaffolding. Therapy gave me language for what my body was doing and permission to pause. A few sessions with a public speaking coach taught me to breathe from somewhere that wasn't panic and to plant my feet like I meant it. I used the skills from my days as a kid at the National Institute of Dramatic Arts, because advocacy is just structured improvisation with consequences; learning to stay present when a conversation zigs instead of zags was invaluable. I practiced with sympathetic audiences – friends, peers, fellow survivor–advocates – so the first time I said a sentence out loud, it wasn't in front of a hostile camera. I built small rituals I could keep even when rattled: a slow inhale for four beats before speaking; a glass of water on the table as a physical anchor; a single sentence I could always return to when I got flustered – 'Here's what this means for survivors.' None of this erased fear, but it made fear survivable.

There's also a line you have to learn to understand and to hold – the difference between useful discomfort and genuine distress. Useful discomfort feels like wobble: butterflies, a heat in your chest, a tremor you can breathe through. It passes after you act. Distress feels like collapse: dissociation, numb hands, tunnel vision, days-long aftershocks. If a room regularly leaves you wired and wrecked, that isn't bravery; that's your body asking you to rethink the tactic. Before I say yes to a hard thing now, I ask, 'Will this help the cause in a way nothing else can? Do I have support and a way to ground afterwards? Am I choosing this from clarity, not obligation or self-punishment?' If I can't answer those cleanly, I reshape the ask – different outlet, different format, different day – or I decline. That isn't weakness. It's strategy. It's also a bridge to what comes in Chapter 8: burnout, boundaries and how to keep going without losing yourself.

You don't have to be fearless to change the world; you just have to be willing to feel the fear and do the thing anyway. Use that fear as fuel. Let the fact that you care so much that it scares you be the very reason you speak up, not an excuse to stay quiet.

When your voice shakes, it doesn't mean you're weak. It means you're speaking from your heart. It means you're challenging something, stretching yourself. And that is powerful. In fact, some of the most powerful words I've uttered came out in a trembling voice with tears in my eyes.

So, embrace the tears, the racing heart and the sweaty palms. Embrace the uncertainty of not knowing exactly what's next. That's life inviting you to show up as your real, raw self, and when you do, you'll tap into a force far greater than comfort ever could offer.

Real change happens when ordinary people dare to step outside their comfort zones and speak truth to power; and that power isn't always a politician or a journalist. Sometimes it's a parent, a boss or a teacher. Finding strength in discomfort has been my greatest superpower, and it's one that every single one of us already holds within, just waiting to be unleashed.

THE SHAKY-VOICE PAGES

Most chapters in this book give you steps and scaffolds. This one asks for something simpler and riskier: your words. Not a perfect speech or a content plan. Just the sentence you need to say out loud, even if your hands tremble when you write it.

Here's how to use the next few pages in your notebook: take a slow breath, then another.

Start with: *I'm here because* ... and keep going until you reach ... *and here's what I'm asking you to do.*

Don't polish. Don't backspace yourself into silence. Tell the truth the way you would if the person who most needs to hear it were sitting across from you.

When you're done, sign the permission slip. It's not legally binding. It's something better: a promise to yourself that you will protect your body and your boundaries while you speak.

What truth are you willing to say out loud, even if your voice shakes?

PERMISSION SLIP TO SPEAK

I give myself permission to speak, even when my voice shakes.

I will protect my boundaries and my body while I do.

Signed: ____________________________________

Date: ______________________________________

The room I will speak in next: ______________________

____

____

Speak, even when your voice shakes.

Chapter 8

BURNOUT ISN'T THE BADGE OF HONOUR YOU THINK IT IS

The work of advocacy can light a fire in your soul, a passionate drive to right wrongs and protect others from the pain you've known. I know I do the work I do to ensure that no other child experiences even a tenth of what I had to. But that same fire can burn you to ash if you're not careful.

It's not just activists who feel it. You don't need a campaign or a cause to run yourself into the ground. It happens to parents who hold everything together for everyone else. To nurses who carry their patients' pain home with them. To people who are constantly the 'strong one' in their family or friend group. Burnout is the dark side of caring deeply – the exhaustion that creeps in after too many long nights, too many heartbreaking stories and too much of yourself poured into a cause without reprieve.

Consider the story of Nialah Edari, who, after months

of protesting racial injustice with her organisation Freedom March NYC, discovered a bald spot forming on her scalp. She was only in her twenties, but her body was already showing physical signs of burnout – hair loss and painful, stress-induced acne. In an interview with Refinery29, she said her body was screaming at her for rest.

Her story is unfortunately not rare. Activists around the world – especially those driven by their own personal trauma – know just how heavy this work can become.

Burnout isn't just 'being tired'. It's physical. It's emotional. It's a slow, creeping exhaustion that steals your joy, your clarity, your sense of meaning. It's what happens when purpose morphs into pressure, and the very thing that once lit you up starts to consume you. When the cause starts draining you instead of fuelling you.

This experience – of feeling hollowed out by the very thing you're most passionate about – isn't new. Back in the 1970s, German–American psychologist Herbert J Freudenberger first defined burnout as 'stress without let-up', a deep emotional depletion that builds up over time until you're left feeling empty. And when you're an advocate, especially one working from lived experience, it's even more complicated, because that exhaustion gets tangled up with trauma. It's not just burnout from working hard, but also from reliving pain over and over again.

Look at climate advocacy: people working for a livable climate – for communities and ecosystems – often describe a particular kind of dismissal from those who haven't felt local impacts yet. They hear versions of 'It's not that bad'; 'Technology will fix it' or 'The market will sort it out.' Many in these spaces report burnout: organisers watching extreme-weather disasters unfold, volunteers witnessing destruction of sea life and coastal habitats all while new coal and gas projects are approved by governments and fossil-fuel companies record billions in profits. Campaigners often say moments such as these are demoralising and add to exhaustion. This isn't 'touchy-feely' overwhelm; it's the strain of holding an urgent, evidence-based risk while parts of the room stay disengaged. Layer survivor-advocacy on top of that, and the load compounds.

Dr Paul Gorski, a scholar of activist burnout, said it clearly: 'All activists put causes above their needs and relationships to a certain degree … That's not the issue. The issue is when they allow their own health and wellbeing to deteriorate because they're doing this to an enormous degree.' In other words, caring about the world isn't the problem; losing yourself to it is.

For many advocates, activism isn't just a job or a political stance – it's personal. Survivors of suffering often become the most passionate advocates for change. The survivor of childhood sexual abuse who campaigns for legal reform. The refugee who speaks out for asylum seekers. The victim of police brutality leading marches against injustice. We carry our lived experience into every petition, every speech, every late-night strategy session. Our personal stories fuel our determination. Being 'trauma-informed' in advocacy means we understand, viscerally, what's at stake. It brings invaluable empathy, perspective and credibility to our work.

And, again, that's the dual edge: when your mission is tied to your own pain, the boundary between your life and your cause thins. The work gets into your nervous system. Over time, that weight accumulates and, if you're not careful, it becomes impossible to carry without consequence.

Even hearing about others' trauma in the same vein can hit like a punch to the gut. As a survivor–advocate working to prevent child sexual abuse and domestic violence, I've had to learn how to ground myself whenever I hear someone else's testimony. There is always a risk that their story may feel like a mirror of my own and brings everything flooding back, triggering flashbacks of my own abuse.

When the work lives in your body, your body remembers what the mind tries to push through. You wake up exhausted even after a full night's sleep. Your chest tightens at the ping of a new email, and your heart races when you see your name tagged online. You're not just tired – you're constantly on edge, wired. Always bracing for the next story, the next ask, the next blow. That's what burnout looks like when it's soaked in trauma. It's not just mental fatigue – it's physical grief.

In a survey of domestic violence and sexual assault advocates based in the United States, researchers found that fifty per cent of advocates in the nonprofit sector were survivors of abuse themselves. That means many who step up to help are carrying their own heavy history. While this shared experience can create a powerful community of survivors and a sense of mission, it also means that the work is never just work – it's intertwined with personal healing and pain. And when your personal identity is so tightly bound to your advocacy, every setback in the cause can feel like a personal defeat, and every story of suffering hits close to home.

What makes this even heavier is the pressure we put on ourselves – and the pressure others put on us – to never falter. Especially when your work is tied to your own survival. You can start to believe that because you've lived through something horrific, you should be able to carry everything that comes after it. That because you've 'made it out', nothing should shake you. You're a survivor now, so act like it. I know that voice well, that push to be strong, to be brave, to be invulnerable, and not just for yourself, but for everyone watching and relying on you. Because when your pain becomes your platform, the expectation to be unbreakable can sneak into the job description. You're not just an advocate anymore; you're an emblem, a symbol of strength. And the moment you crack? People question the cause.

Here's a quick distinction that's helped me.

Pain as platform is when the wound itself is the stage. You're asked (or feel compelled) to perform your pain over and over to prove the need is real. That keeps the wound open and increases burnout risk.

Pain as purpose is different. It's letting what happened inform your direction, then building systems, boundaries and community so you're not constantly re-bleeding. You speak from scar tissue, not open wounds. That shift lowers the temperature. It doesn't magic away the cost, but it does help prevent burnout because you're orienting to transformation, not reproduction of harm.

We see the 'unbreakable emblem' pressure play out all the time. A prominent climate organiser pauses for mental health and critics crow that the 'movement is collapsing'. A women's safety advocate admits to needing a break and the trolls call it hypocrisy. Disability advocates who disclose sensory overwhelm get mocked for asking for accessible formats. The message beneath those pile-ons is always the same: *be tireless or be dismissed.* It's dehumanising – and it's also a lie. Movements are healthiest when their leaders rest.

Families are no different. The people who hold everything together, whether it's a cause or a home, deserve to step back and breathe. Because when you rest, everything you've built has a chance to breathe with you.

Psychologists call one slice of this compassion fatigue – and yes, it shows up beyond activists. Front-line caseworkers, first responders, emergency medicine professionals, teachers, carers, and engaged supporters who are not capital-A activists can feel it too. When injustices feel multiple and insurmountable, anyone who keeps their heart open can hit a wall. It's your nervous system saying, 'I need a breather.'

Constant exposure to trauma – whether direct or vicarious – can echo post-traumatic stress: chronic insomnia, hypervigilance, headaches, anxiety, a weakened immune system. Activists frequently report these symptoms in ways similar to first responders and emergency medicine staff. Witnessing harm repeatedly, even on screens, wires your brain to expect danger. Your worldview can warp. One day you're raging at injustice; the next you're crying at 2am, replaying a gut-wrenching story and bracing for the next one. If that goes on long enough, pain hardens into cynicism. Hope thins and motivation wobbles. You catch yourself thinking, *Maybe nothing ever changes.*

That's the descent into numbness I described earlier. It's your brain putting up safety barriers after too much. And when your identity is built on care, going numb feels terrifying, like a betrayal of who you are. You feel guilty, like you're failing the cause. But the truth is, your body is pulling an emergency brake. You're not broken; you're saturated.

Social media adds another layer. As we established in Chapter 6, it's where movements are built, but also where advocates get shredded. Trolls, abuse, character assassinations, doxxing and death threats are alarmingly common, especially if you're a woman, a person of colour, a member of the LGBTQ+ community or from a religious minority. One global study from Amnesty International found that three in five young activists have been harassed online for doing nothing more than sharing human rights content. Imagine being seventeen and getting death threats for sharing a post.

For survivors, it can be deeply triggering. Reading a barrage of hateful comments doesn't just cause stress – it can activate trauma. Especially when the insults echo the exact words of past abusers. Suddenly, your phone becomes a panic button. Your hands shake when you open Instagram, and you flinch when your name lights up in a notification because your brain has learned that this might hurt. That constant vigilance transforms the very tool you use to uplift others into a conduit for hate, a direct line for abuse right into your pocket.

Sometimes, this rhetoric doesn't come from just strangers or trolls but your own community: advocates turning on advocates not over values, but over tone, tactics, clout or who said the wrong thing in 2013. What starts as accountability becomes something else entirely – call-outs spiral into pile-ons, DMs turn into minefields and the people you once stood beside are now sub-tweeting you into silence.

This is called lateral violence: when people within a

marginalised community turn on one another, often out of unhealed trauma, internalised oppression or the pressure to be perfect. It shows up as gossip, gatekeeping, public shaming and quiet exclusion, especially in close-knit circles where everyone knows everyone and no one wants to be next. It hurts in a different kind of way – not because you can't take criticism, but because you expected solidarity. Instead, you get silence. Or worse, friendly fire. You start to question where you're actually safe, because when both the outside world and your own community feel like war zones, there's no room to breathe.

I've also seen the opposite – and it kept people in. When we first got involved with one particular activist organisation, there was an amazing culture of acceptance. Every person's capacity for involvement was respected, and no one questioned anyone choosing to step into something or step back. It was clear each activist could be trusted to participate to the extent of their ability, and only they could define that extent. It made it so easy to put your hand up.

It didn't stay that way for long, and look, I understand. People are desperate. They want progress. But once suspicion crept in, once the vibe shifted to 'prove you care by doing more', it turned toxic and drove many people out.

Bottom line: treat volunteers (and employees) like adults who do what they can. Assume good faith. Capacity fluctuates. Trust people to know theirs.

It's really no surprise that so many advocates burn out, or disappear altogether. It's not because they stopped caring, but because the internet made caring a full-time, unpaid, trauma-repeating job. As we've established, social media is an extra layer of emotional labour that previous generations of activists didn't face. Of course, activists have always faced criticism and internal disputes, but the scale and intensity now is unprecedented. A misstep or a controversial stance can unleash hundreds of attacking messages overnight. Public visibility also means activists feel pressure to maintain a certain image or to constantly educate others on social media, which is a massive effort in itself – particularly for advocates from marginalised groups being asked to 'explain your pain' over and over, or to calmly educate those who deny your reality. It's incredibly taxing.

Burnout isn't just emotional – it is an all-encompassing, multidimensional state. It can seep into your body, your thoughts, your relationships, your habits and yes, even your bank account. It reshapes the way you live.

One of the most overlooked dimensions of burnout in advocacy is financial strain. This work doesn't come with a salary, and on the rare occasion it does, it's rarely enough. Even when a speaking engagement or panel appearance pops up, payment is often uncertain. Activism is always seen as a *charitable act* because of its nature, as if emotional labour somehow isn't real labour. Organisations and government bodies seem to forget that they need us more than we need them and we're often thanked with vouchers, gift cards or 'exposure', when what we actually deserve is proper, legitimate, substantial monetary payment. It's blatant exploitation dressed up as gratitude and an 'opportunity to network'.

Think about what it takes: the hours spent writing a speech, preparing yourself for disclosures from audience members after you talk, and the emotional aftermath of pouring your absolute heart out on a stage in front of strangers. That isn't charity, that's hard fucking work. Work that deserves compensation, boundaries, and recovery time. And when institutions fail to recognise that, they're reinforcing the same power imbalances we're trying to dismantle. Many of us are volunteers, casual workers or juggling side jobs to stay afloat while pouring hours into unpaid organising. We pay for printing flyers, take unpaid leave to attend meetings and spend evenings choosing between groceries and campaign materials. We give everything we have – sometimes quite literally.

Chronic financial stress doesn't just weigh you down; it amplifies burnout. You're trying to fight a system while barely keeping yourself upright. You turn down stable careers because they clash with your values. You spend your savings on interstate travel to speak at rallies and meet with politicians. You skip therapy because it's way too expensive, then spiral because you're not coping. And when burnout finally knocks you down, you might not have the safety net to catch you.

I know this reality intimately. Over the years, I've turned down jobs worth over $100,000 each year because I wanted to keep focusing on campaigning. Roles that would've offered me stability, security and a clean, predictable life, but would've pulled me away from the fight. Instead, I poured schooners behind a bar until 2am, delivered Uber Eats in my fiancée's car to cover rent and took out personal loans. All to keep going.

In 2024, I found myself stepping through the gates of Admiralty House, a place that's hosted royal family members, popes and presidents – to meet with Governor-General Sam Mostyn. I had just $17 in my bank account.

On the outside, I looked like someone who had it all together – dressed in my nicest navy-blue Australian wool suit, wearing my grandfather's vintage eighties Christian Dior tie and boots I'd polished the night before. I looked like someone who belonged in that room. But on the inside, I felt like I was barely holding it together.

I was there representing survivors on National Survivors' Day, as one of the 2024 ambassadors, being congratulated for my advocacy. The governor-general couldn't have been more gracious. I remember asking her what life was like now that she'd stepped into the role, and she smiled and said, 'Shopping for groceries has become rather difficult.'

She guided a small group of us – survivor–advocates – through Admiralty House, pointing out the artwork on the walls with genuine pride. You could tell she adored it – not just for how it looked, but for what it represented. Every piece was Australian, carefully chosen and curated by her. She knew the stories behind each brushstroke, the names of the artists, the meaning woven into the canvas. It wasn't just decoration; it was our culture, our history, our national identity.

Then, as we stood in her sunlit office overlooking the harbour, she turned to us – a group of people who had endured unimaginable pain, some of us still shaking off the impostor syndrome we'd carried through the gates – and said softly, but with complete conviction, 'This house is your house. You are always welcome here.'

It wasn't just a polite gesture. In that moment, it felt like something rare – recognition, dignity and belonging, spoken in a place that had never felt built for people like us.

But while I was shaking hands and smiling for photos, I was also quietly calculating whether I could afford the train ride home. I hadn't eaten lunch – I couldn't afford to. I was devouring the sandwiches and biscuits served at morning tea not out of politeness, but out of necessity. I was deep in conversation with 2025 Australian of the Year nominees and university professors, nodding and laughing along while silently wondering how far I could stretch the last few dollars in my account.

That wasn't rock bottom – well, not technically – but it was close enough to feel the weight of it.

And that's the part no one tells you about burnout.

It doesn't always look like collapse. It doesn't always announce itself with alarm bells and flashing warning signs. Sometimes, it wears a tailored suit and delivers speeches to a room full of powerful people. Sometimes it comes dressed as success. I was being publicly praised for my resilience and impact while being financially, physically and emotionally spent.

Somewhere along the way, the work stopped being something I did and started becoming who I was, my name, my story, my worth all fused into the cause. I didn't notice it at first – it felt like passion, a calling – but eventually, the edges started to blur. I wasn't Harrison anymore, I was 'the kid who fucked his stepmother'; 'the survivor'; 'the campaigner'.

And when things didn't go to plan – when a campaign stalled, when support dried up, when I couldn't hold it all together – I felt defective, like I had failed not just the cause, but myself.

That's the trickiest part of burnout. It's not just exhaustion but distortion. It makes it hard to tell where the work ends and where you begin. It whispers that you are only as valuable as your output and that rest is weakness.

If your activism is rooted in trauma – if you're not just fighting for something but from something – that pressure multiplies. The line between healing and helping becomes paper-thin. And I stopped knowing which one I was trying to do.

I developed a quiet saviour complex, building my self-worth around being the one who could fix things, help others, be the voice for the voiceless. Helping others gave me purpose, and for a while, it helped me cope with my own trauma by focusing on everyone else's. When something went wrong, I didn't just feel disappointment, I felt shame, like I had failed everyone and myself. When your identity is built around saving the day, anything short of that can feel like a personal indictment. Over time, that constant pressure morphs into bitterness. You start thinking, *I gave everything … and it still wasn't enough. Maybe I'm not enough.* That pain is soul-deep. The rage. The disillusionment. The quiet resentment that builds when you give everything to a cause – and start to wonder what's left for you.

If you're not careful, this work will hollow you out. But, slowly, I began to arrive at a truth that changed everything: to sustain others, you must first sustain yourself.

Advocacy is not a sprint, it's a marathon, and the most passionate change-makers are often the most at risk of losing themselves. This is not because they don't care, but because they care so much, so deeply, for so long. The great news is that those same people, with the right tools and boundaries, are also the ones who can learn to thrive without extinguishing their fire.

If it sounds like I'm complaining about advocacy, I'm not. This is the path I chose with my eyes wide open and, despite everything I've just shared, I still choose it – every single day.

But the way I choose it now looks very different to how it used to. I no longer measure my worth by how much I sacrifice. I don't say yes to everything. I've learned that boundaries don't make me selfish – they make me sustainable.

Some days, advocacy looks like speaking at Parliament House or writing a submission for a review or supporting another survivor through a crisis behind the scenes. Other days, it looks like closing the laptop, putting my phone on silent and going for a walk while I hold hands with my fiancée. It looks like building a life that isn't just about fighting, but about living, too.

THE BURNOUT FIELD GUIDE (FOR ANYONE TRYING TO MAKE THINGS BETTER WITHOUT LOSING THEMSELVES)

This is the practical bit I needed at the start of my advocacy journey. Use it however you need: as a quiet audit, a plan you share with your team or a note on your fridge. It's written for advocates, organisers, supporters and anyone who loves something enough to lose themselves in it.

1. **Name your pattern (answer honestly, three sentences for each).**

   When have you felt burnt-out before? What were the tells (sleep, irritability, numbness, scrolling, aches, dread)?

   ____

   ____

   ____

   ____

   How did you recover last time? What actually helped (time off, therapy, sunlight, saying no, different tasks, deleting apps, money help)?

   ____

   ____

   ____

   ____

2. **Prevention – building the guardrails (what I do differently today)**

   Capacity is a number, not a vibe. Pick a weekly ceiling (e.g. eight hours of advocacy outside paid work or two night events a month). Jot it down below. Put it in your calendar. Tell someone who'll keep you honest.

   ____

   ____

   ____

   ____

   Boundaries that survive a bad day. In your notebook, write some lines you'll need when you're tired. For example:

   'I can't give this the attention it deserves right now.'

   'My capacity is full this week; try me next fortnight.'

   'I don't discuss my trauma in DMs. Here are three services that can hold you properly.'

   Try these or implement these exercises into your advocacy plan:

   Role rotation. If you share an organisation or campaign like Jarad and I, rotate hot-zone duties (media, triage, moderating) every two to four weeks so no one becomes the permanent sponge.

   Digital hygiene. Notifications off by default; app-free hours nightly; 'post and walk' for heavy content; zero doom-scrolling in bed.

Body basics as policy. A regular sleep schedule, actual food, water, movement you don't hate. Put one joyful thing in the week that has nothing to do with the cause.

Money plan. Name what you can afford to give (time and cash). Build a tiny 'campaign kitty' line in your budget so emergencies don't wipe you out.

Community of care. Identify three humans: a peer (gets the work), a friend (doesn't need details) and a pro (therapist/GP). Save their numbers.

If you're a part of a team, an organisation or even just a family, create a Culture Pledge, something like: 'We treat capacity as self-defined; pauses are respected; no shaming for stepping back.' Put it in writing and make sure everyone is familiar with it.

3. **If it's too late – acute recovery (the seventy-two-hour reset)**

If you've already hit the wall – the exhaustion, the tears in the shower, the 'I can't do this anymore' moment – this is where you start. You can't fix burnout overnight, but you can interrupt it. Think of the next seventy-two hours as a reset window where your only job is to stabilise your body and quiet your nervous system. Consider these tips and how you could utilise them in practical terms for your lifestyle:

Call it. Say, out loud: 'I'm burnt out.' Pausing is cheaper than breaking.

Stop the bleed. Cancel non-essential tasks. Hand over live items with one paragraph and a deadline. Put up an auto-reply with crisis lines and a return date.

Regulate, then reflect. For three days, prioritise sleep, food, sun, gentle movement and zero comment sections. No 'catching up'. No self-pep-talks. Just nervous system care.

Name the drivers. After the fog lifts a little, write the three forces that cooked you (money, DMs, pile-ons, grief, over-functioning). For each, choose one counter-move you will actually do.

Cancel what you can. Turn your phone off for a few hours. Eat something with actual nutrition. Drink water. Sleep, even if it's broken. Get sunlight. Do one small thing that brings you back into yourself. You're not fixing your life here; you're giving your body a signal that it's safe to slow down. Once you've done that for three days, you can start thinking about the bigger repair work.

4. **Maintenance.**

   Consider a quarterly reflection. Once a season: what work lights me up? What work drains me? What can I delegate? What will I stop (or put on a ninety-day hold)? Reflect on the prompts below in your notebook:

   Consider reframing from 'pain as platform' to 'pain as purpose'. Build systems that let you contribute without constantly reopening the wound: anonymised case studies, policy work, training others. What would this look like to you?

What are some rituals that you could implement in your daily routine to help close the day? After heavy work: shower, walk, cook or stretch to tell your body the danger has passed. Tiny, repeatable closures matter. What does that look like?

CHOOSING TO LAST

I still show up. I still care, deeply. But I've stopped letting that care consume me. I've learned to protect the parts of me that exist outside the cause – the loving partner, the loyal friend, the talented artist who draws cartoons, the person who laughs and sleeps and eats well and sometimes does absolutely nothing of any strategic value at all.

Choosing advocacy doesn't have to mean choosing burnout, and choosing to protect your energy doesn't mean you've stopped making a difference. If anything, it means you're in it for the long haul. It means you're making this sustainable – not just for yourself, but for everyone who's watching you, wondering if they can do this work and still stay whole. 'Rest is activism,' a dear friend once told me. 'It's what fuels us for the moments that matter most – the times where we really need to show up.'

I'm not telling you any of this to scare you off or to make you feel sorry for me. I want to offer a realistic picture of what to expect, because no one ever gave me that; and if you know what's coming, you can actually prepare for it.

Advocacy can be deeply fulfilling. It can connect you with people you never would've met, give your pain a purpose, and lead to real, lasting change that benefits the lives of many like you. But it can also suck the soul out of you, if you're not careful. It can leave you burnt out, bitter and wondering where your life went.

Do I recommend becoming an activist? Not in the same way I'd recommend a nice restaurant or a series on Netflix to binge-watch. But I also have no right to talk you out of it. If something's burning in your chest, if injustice keeps you up at night, if you've been nodding along to the pages in this book, then we both already know you'll do it anyway. Because you have to. Because, like me, you'll probably feel like you don't have a choice.

And that's why I'm telling you all this. You picked up this book because you've known pain – your own, or someone else's – and you're ready to do something with it. However you define that 'something', I hope these pages have helped you see that change begins with you. But it would be negligent of me not to tell you what I know: burnout is fucked, and it is real. That the toll can be heavy, and protecting yourself is a necessity. So let this be that warning, but let it also be permission. To rest. To heal. To build a life alongside the fight. Because the world needs all of you, not just the parts that serve the cause.

I have come to realise that I have permission to be a whole, healthy human. In fact, more than that – I have a responsibility to be one. Because taking care of my body, my mind, my happiness, my peace is not only sensible, it's strategic.

By caring for yourself, you're able to model sustainable activism for everyone who comes after you. You show new advocates that they don't have to choose between making a difference and having a life. They can do both, if they set boundaries, build community and treat their wellbeing as part of the movement. Because as advocates, we fight so that others can enjoy safety, peace and fulfilment. We must remember to grant ourselves a slice of that peace, too.

Imagine an advocacy community that celebrates not just wins such as passing a bill or publishing a story, but also personal milestones such as taking a holiday, going to therapy, healing from burnout or saying no without guilt.

That kind of culture is already beginning to emerge. Words like 'regenerative activism', 'trauma-informed organising' and 'collective care' are gaining traction, because people are realising that a movement full of burnt-out individuals is unsustainable. But a movement full of healthy, supported, rested people? That's a force of nature.

So please – as you fight for what you love, don't forget to protect your own heart, too. Your passion brought you here. And with care, it can carry you for a lifetime.

Chapter 9

SCALE YOUR MISSION BUILT ON HEART

When Jarad and I launched #YourReferenceAintRelevant in New South Wales in May 2023, we had no illusions about how tough this was going to be. We did have momentum – media attention, growing public interest, meetings starting to happen with politicians across the country, both state and federal – and a feeling that the conversation was finally moving. Sitting in a small cafe after those first glimmers of traction, we asked each other the question that changes a project into a movement: how do we scale this across Australia without compromising the soul of it – or ourselves?

We agreed on one thing immediately: if we grew, we would grow by sharing the platform, not hoarding it. That wasn't just a tactic, it was a responsibility. From the beginning, the beating heart of the campaign was survivors telling the truth about what it feels like to sit in court, hear an abuser praised for their 'good character' and watch that praise dilute the harm. If #YourReferenceAintRelevant expanded, it had to expand with lived-experience leadership at the centre in each state and territory. Real stories, real people, real stakes. We didn't want this to become a brand exercise. We wanted it to stay human.

And we wanted to model something for anyone reading this: don't be afraid to share your platform. Campaigns built on genuine heart and genuine stories bring everyday people – the masses – on board. They see themselves in the faces and voices they recognise as 'one of us'. That's how you grow pressure without losing trust.

Even if you're not leading a campaign, there's a version of this that matters just as much in everyday life. It's about surrounding yourself with people who meet you with empathy – friends, colleagues and partners who listen, who ask instead of assume, and who hold your story gently. In a way, that's its own kind of movement: building a personal network made up of people who are trauma-informed, compassionate and safe. You can't create change, or even heal properly, if you're constantly bracing for harm. Whether you're building a campaign or a circle of trust, the principle is the same: find the ones who see you, not just the version of you who helps them.

THE ACT: WHEN ONE VOICE BECAME MANY

Our first test of this 'share the platform' approach came in late 2023 in the Australian Capital Territory. Through survivor networks we met Josh Byrnes, a Canberra local, a husband and a new dad with a harrowing story and a steady conviction that made you want to sit up straighter.

Josh was groomed and sexually abused by a relative – a Catholic priest – throughout his adolescence. When that priest was finally prosecuted, Josh learned how easily the system can still be swayed by 'good character' praise. 'I had a lifetime of people telling me this man was amazing, and that he was kind,' he reflected in an interview, describing how character talk creates cover for harm. In his case, the perpetrator's position as clergy prevented him from using character references, because he was considered a figure of authority under law. But Josh knew that, in many other cases, abusers can exploit personal references to seek leniency. 'If it wasn't for the fact that he was a parish priest, there's a chance he would've been able to use character references to potentially minimise his sentence,' he said. 'I don't think that's right. I don't think there should be absolutely any leniency whatsoever for this crime. Sexual abuse is the worst of the worst.'

Josh wasn't angling for the spotlight; he was angling for a safer country for his kid. It was the exact voice we wanted front and centre. So, in October 2023, we launched #YourReferenceAintRelevant in the ACT, with Josh as the local champion, standing together on the steps of the ACT Legislative Assembly with a simple, precise ask: amend the *Crimes (Sentencing) Act 2005* to close the loophole that left room for good character references in certain child sexual abuse cases, because no survivor should ever have to hear their abuser's reputation weighed against their trauma. Ever.

The ACT took us seriously. Attorney-General Shane Rattenbury met with us and with Josh soon after the petition launched, bringing a warmth and a people-first approach that cuts through cynicism. It wasn't lip-service. He thanked us for the spotlight and acknowledged the harm of good character references on victim–survivors. He convened a roundtable with justice stakeholders and directed his department to research options, with a report due within months. Crucially, he didn't keep it local; he took the issue national, requesting it on the agenda for the next meeting of the nation's attorneys-general. From that point, every state and territory – along with the then federal attorney-general, Mark Dreyfus – was informed of our work. Both NSW and the ACT formally put on record that they had initiated reviews into the matter, and it granted the campaign opportunities for us to meet with other jurisdictions across the country.

That was monumental. You can campaign for years and never get your issue spoken aloud in the right room. Seeing 'abolish good character references in child sexual abuse sentencing' listed alongside national law reform priorities felt surreal.

As I mentioned in Chapter 4, the NSW and the ACT reviews are now the ones to watch. The other jurisdictions are paying attention and, in different ways, waiting to see how those processes land. That is exactly how systems move: a few places lead, momentum builds, others follow. Our job as campaigners is to keep the pressure and the story human while those cogs turn.

SOUTH AUSTRALIA: WHEN ALYSSA SPOKE, A STATE LISTENED

We turned to South Australia in mid-2024, ready to expand if we found the right person. We found our leader on the ground in Alyssa James, a mother of two from Adelaide whose story still punches me in the chest.

When Alyssa was six, a family member she should've been able to trust sexually abused her. Years later, when that person finally went to court, Alyssa suffered a second betrayal: her own parents wrote glowing character references for the perpetrator. One called him a 'valued member of the community'. Those references influenced the judge, and the family member walked free with a suspended sentence and no conviction recorded.

'I cannot stress enough how horrific it was,' Alyssa told us. 'The impact of hearing people excuse what he did to me, to diminish it by speaking about his good character, was hugely traumatic.' Out of that devastation, she found resolve. 'I don't want another human being to go through that, to feel so deserted and invalidated by our legal system.' She said yes to leading the South Australian campaign without hesitation, sharing her story publicly for the first time. Pure bravery.

We launched #YourReferenceAintRelevant in South Australia in July 2024 with a clear focus: Section 11(4) of the *Sentencing Act 2017*. The ask was familiar: end the use of character references for convicted child sexual offenders. Alyssa spoke to local and national media, and her plain-spoken line – 'Who cares if a child abuser is a nice guy?' – cut through legal abstractions like a scalpel.

South Australia's attorney-general, Kyam Maher, met with us and responded with the same human-first approach we'd seen in the ACT. He publicly voiced support for reform and set his office to examining the legislative path. Again: partnership, not performance. We walked into that office as advocates and walked out as collaborators.

If there's one idea I want you to hold here, it's this: scaling with integrity means stepping back so others can step forward, especially when they carry perspectives you don't. Jarad and I could have tried to front the South Australian push with our own voices, but it would not have landed like Alyssa's did. Her story anchored the ask in South Australian lives. And that's not us 'using' stories; that's us refusing to replace them with talking points. The result didn't feel like an outsider campaign landing in Adelaide – it felt home-grown, because it was.

THE NEXT SET OF STATES

We then turned toward Western Australia, Tasmania, Victoria and Queensland. Each has a distinct political landscape and community rhythm, and each will need reform in its own way.

Finding survivors who felt ready to go public proved difficult. That's not a judgment about those places; it's a reflection of how personal risk and public stigma operate for many people, and how varied support networks can be. From our vantage point – and I'm being careful here – we simply didn't yet have local partners willing or able to carry the public load. We respected those boundaries.

Instead, we used the tools we had. We pitched, we wrote, we took interviews, we shared updates and law-in-plain-English from other states to prime the conversation. Those launches were quieter, but that doesn't mean they didn't matter. Quiet can soften the ground for the moment when a local leader steps up, the government is ready to move and the reviews from other states are in.

There were weeks where Jarad and I divided and conquered, with one flying to a meeting while the other kept media plates spinning. We were tired and grateful in equal measure. And there were moments when I stepped back and noticed the shift: a niche legal practice – character references in child sexual abuse cases – was becoming a mainstream conversation. A thing that was whispered about in courts was now being argued at kitchen tables around the country. More people were joining the conversation.

That might sound scary. If you're afraid scaling will strip your cause of intimacy, don't be. If you scale by making room for more real people, rather than filling every room yourself, the heart of your campaign gets bigger.

CREATING A GUIDE FOR SCALING WITH HEART

I wish someone had handed me a page and said: 'Here's how to invite lived-experience leaders in with care. Here's how to build a team that burns bright without burning out. Here's how to grow without losing the plot.' So that's what I'm giving you.

Read this next section as part how-to, part promise. It will help you bring lived-experience leadership into your campaign with care and build a wider team that shares your fire. Leave space in your notebook to reflect on these tips for where you're going and how you'll get there.

Inviting lived-experience leaders in (without extracting them)

Lead with consent and clarity. Your first message isn't 'Can you tell your story?' It's 'Here's the change we're pushing for, why it matters and the ways someone with lived experience could lead if and when it feels right for them.' Spell out time asks, media expectations, safety considerations and the right to say no at any point.

Offer roles, not a script. Some people will want to front the media. Others will prefer closed-door briefings with decision-makers or shaping messaging behind the scenes. Lay out options. Let them choose. Revisit that choice often. Always respect people's autonomy.

Co-design support from day one. Together, build a wellbeing plan: preferred press hours, off-limit topics, a buddy for debriefs, an opt-out phrase for interviews, boundaries around comments and DMs. Put crisis services and legal support in one shared note you can both access.

Compensate where you can. Stipends, honoraria, travel, childcare. If the budget is zero, be honest and keep looking for funds. Payment doesn't cheapen authenticity; it honours labour and risk.

Name the power dynamics out loud. 'We don't want to "use" your story. We want to build with you, at your pace, on your terms. We'll check in frequently, because relying on someone who's been conditioned to stay silent and expecting them to speak up isn't fair. If it ever feels extractive, we'll stop, listen and repair.'

Build a wider team that shares the fire

Write a one-page 'why' – your campaign's heartbeat in plain language. The harm, the fix, the non-negotiables and the way you treat each other. Everyone new reads it, comments and signs off. It can always be used to mediate disagreements if they ever arise.

Create clear lanes: media, policy, community outreach, survivor care, operations. Invite people into lanes that fit their skills and capacity. Cross-train lightly so no one becomes a single point of failure.

Normalise capacity. Make it culture to say, 'I can give four hours this week,' or 'I need two weeks off.' Treat volunteers like adults who will do what they can, when they can. Praise the handover as much as the heroics.

Celebrate small wins. A meeting secured, a line changed in a draft, a parent who wrote to say thank you. These are fuel. Name them in the group chat. Momentum loves measurement, but it also loves meaning.

Keep expansion human, local and effective

Local anchor, national frame. Keep the core ask consistent ('End character references for convicted child sexual offenders'), while letting the local champion shape language and outreach. It's their community. Listen to them, thank them for their expertise and appreciate their insight.

Find your people-first allies. The right official can cut months off a process. Look for those who speak (and act) like humans. Offer them partnership, not pressure. If they pass, the public-pressure route is still there.

Treat all media like a bridge, not a bonfire. Be open, honest, precise. Don't try to win the news cycle; try to earn trust. Put lived-experience voices up front by choice, not by default. Protect them when the room gets hot.

Keep a living timeline. One shared doc with: status by jurisdiction, who's doing what, next procedural steps and any risks. Clarity calms nerves and prevents duplication.

REFLECTION PAGES

Take your time here. Use pages in your notebook to write in, to return to and to update as your campaign or personal mission grows.

1. **Who could lead with you?**
   Name three people with lived experience or community credibility in your issue area. For each, write why you thought of them, what role they might choose, and what support they'd need.

2. **Your non-negotiables.**
   List the values you will not trade for reach or speed. (e.g. 'Survivor safety over media urgency.')

3. **Your lanes and your limits.**
   Where are you most useful? Where will you step back? What's your weekly capacity – truly?

4. **Your two-sentence pitch (local + national).**

   Write the harm and fix in your local dialect, then write the same in a national frame.

GROW WITH INTEGRITY

Scaling this movement taught me that integrity and impact aren't opposites. You can grow wide and stay close. You can move faster without rushing people. You can hand the mic over and make the message louder.

It taught me that 'national force to be reckoned with' is a headline, not a goal. The goal is simply this: no survivor should ever hear an abuser praised in the same breath a court considers their harm. Every step toward that is a win. Every person who joins makes the step easier.

I want to acknowledge what this actually looked like on the ground. We had weeks of back-to-back media hits and months where it felt like we were pushing fog uphill. We had the gift of people-first attorneys-general in the ACT and South Australia, and we had polite versions of 'not yet' elsewhere. We had flights and emails and late-night debriefs and mornings where I stared at my phone, wondering if I'd said the right thing yesterday. We had a lot of 'thank you for your advocacy' and some 'who do you think you are?'. We had a handful of trolls and an ocean of kindness. And threading through all of it, we had survivors choosing to be heard.

If you're carrying a cause right now, I hope you read this chapter and walk away with two things: the confidence that you can scale without losing yourself, and the tools to bring other people in without losing them.

To Josh and Alyssa – thank you, not just for lending your voices to this campaign, but for offering your hearts, your stories and your strength in the moments it mattered most. From the day you each stepped forward, this campaign became something far bigger than a policy change – it became a movement rooted in truth, dignity and the unshakable courage of survivors willing to speak up not just for themselves, but for all those still sitting in silence.

Josh, your quiet determination and unwavering clarity have left a lasting mark. You brought a sense of integrity and calm strength that anchored our ACT launch and reminded everyone that this was never about outrage – it was about justice. You never sought the spotlight, yet when it found you, you carried it with grace. The way you spoke – not with rehearsed slogans, but with honesty, clarity and the lived reality of someone who had endured and overcome – changed minds. You shifted public discourse. You opened doors. You proved that lived experience is essential for policy reform. Thank you for trusting us with your story, for walking this road with us, and for reminding survivors everywhere that they are not alone.

Alyssa, your bravery has been nothing short of revolutionary. In sharing a story so personal, so raw and so painful – especially in a state where silence around child sexual abuse has long prevailed – you didn't just speak truth to power, you cracked something open. You gave other survivors permission to feel their pain, to speak their own truths and to demand better. The dignity and fire with which you told your story shook the foundations of how people think about justice. You reminded everyone that character references aren't just a legal technicality – they're a slap in the face to those who've already survived the unthinkable. Your strength has been magnetic, pulling this campaign forward when we needed it most. You've inspired thousands, whether they've told you so or not.

Together, Josh and Alyssa, you became the heart of this campaign. In a world where political debates are often reduced to noise and numbers, you brought humanity. You showed that real people live in the shadow of these laws, and real people are harmed when the system gets it wrong. Most importantly, you showed that real people can change it. You stood up. You stood firm. And because of that, we're seeing a shift that is no longer just possible – it's inevitable.

On a personal level, I am endlessly grateful to both of you – for your time, your trust, your presence and your patience. For every interview, every signature collected, every media moment navigated and every difficult day endured for the sake of this cause. For your texts, your phone calls, your late-night reflections. For carrying this with us. Your involvement hasn't just made this campaign stronger, it made it grounded in reality and that's what people connect to. That's what changes the world.

If we – an architect, a dad, a mum and a young bloke pouring beers on weekends – could do this, so can you. Start where you are. Find the person in your community whose story needs the mic, and offer them the stand, the glass of water and the promise that you'll hold the door while they speak. Keep your non-negotiables close. Build rest into the plan. And when the room opens, walk in together.

My team at the campaign remind me constantly that advocacy isn't something we do alone; it's something we build together. So maybe take a moment to think about who you want to thank, too. The people who showed up for you. The ones who made you braver, steadier or softer. Because movements don't just run on strategy, they run on gratitude.

And that's how you scale a mission built on heart, even if your mission is simply making your life, and the lives of those around you, safe and loved. You don't make it bigger by building walls; you make it bigger by letting more people in.

Chapter 10

INSTEAD OF CHANGING LIVES, START LIVING ONE

I don't think it would be honest to end this book on a neat, triumphant note. Not because there hasn't been triumph, and not because I'm allergic to happiness, but because pretending everything ties up with a clean ribbon would be kind of disrespectful to the truth of survivors' lives, to the relentlessness of the work and to the stubborn complexity of trying to make anything better while the world keeps breaking in new places. We live with the consequences of our abusers' actions every day. We carry them into rooms where no one else can see them; we carry them in our chests when we misinterpret a conversation that feels like conflict; we carry them into friendships and work and love. There's no switch you can flip that makes it simple. Healing is never linear. Justice gets delayed or diluted or denied. Closure is a luxury most of us don't get.

And the world is still deeply, relentlessly fucked.

Children are still being sexually abused. Survivors are still being sidelined, disbelieved or used up for their stories and then left to patch themselves alone. Misogynists, warmongers and straight-up fuckwits are still being elected to positions of power. Genocide is unfolding in plain sight, with entire communities wiped out while the world argues over semantics and timelines. The gap between left and right grows wider, with people being radicalised online faster than we can build bridges. Women's rights are being stripped back under the banner of 'traditional values'. Queer and trans people are being scapegoated to stir fear and win votes. Courts still shield perpetrators. The planet is burning, flooding and choking with fire seasons that never end, rivers that can't breathe and oceans coughing up dead fish while leaders debate whether now is the 'right time' to act. People seeking safety across borders are treated like policy problems more than human beings. Truth itself is under attack, rewritten and repackaged as propaganda. We're consuming more than we'll ever need, forgetting that what actually sustains us isn't stuff – it's each other.

Wherever you look – in health, housing, climate, justice or even basic decency – there's a ledger of harm that doesn't balance just because we want it to.

I've sat in the corridors of parliament, watching the minutes slide by while urgent things get rebranded as 'complex' or 'under review'. I've stood in court foyers where the air feels too thin and waited in media green rooms while someone checks make-up on a panellist who plans to say survivors are 'exaggerating' or aggressors are merely acting in 'self-defence'. Moments like these will certainly test your faith in humanity, and it'll be really easy to give into pessimism and divisiveness – trust me, I've felt it. I know happy endings are never guaranteed. They are sometimes possible, sometimes partial and often invisible to anyone outside the handful of people whose lives have actually shifted.

But in a world that is so often cruel, being kind, showing empathy and holding onto hope are all revolutionary acts. And I believe – with everything in me – that it's possible to end this book on a realistically hopeful note.

Hope isn't naive, or a pastel filter you throw over wreckage. The kind of hope I recognise is heavier, deliberate. It's the decision to look at what is, name it without flinching and still choose to move. It's refusing to outsource your conscience to the news cycle. It's the daily practice of accepting the hard fucking work that's ahead and saying: *Yes, this hurts and yes, it's complicated and yes, it's bigger than me – and also, I can take responsibility for my square metre of earth. I can show up where my feet are. I can make a dent.*

The older I get, the more I understand that hope is less about adrenaline and more about discipline; less about the perfect strategy and more about the imperfect presence that keeps showing up, especially when no one is clapping or even watching.

If you'd told me as a thirteen-year-old kid – sick with fear, learning how to fold my body around danger in ways that looked like 'coping' – that I would one day help spark national conversations about justice, I would've stared at you like you'd got the wrong person. If you'd said I'd stand in rooms with ministers and ask for what survivors in the community need, or call out a network live on air, or walk through Admiralty

House with a sunlit Sydney Harbour staring back at me, I would have thought you were mixing me up with someone else. Yet here we are.

I've watched petitions multiply into meetings, meetings turn into reviews and reviews edge closer to laws; I've seen everyday people decide that 'ordinary' is a lie we were sold and that their voice counts. I've met my heroes and realised they're just people who kept at it. I've stood next to strangers who became family because we told the truth side by side. What humbles me most is how often the spark was small: a message from someone who'd never spoken aloud what happened to them, a local paper that ran a story when bigger outlets wouldn't, a volunteer who showed up after work and stayed late into the night to help just one more person. My life is a case study in this sentence that I need you to believe: we all have far more influence than we tend to give ourselves credit for.

Influence is defined as having an effect on the way that someone behaves or thinks, especially by giving them an example to follow. We all possess that power. Influence isn't fireworks; it's answering the message, or skipping Friday night drinks so you can show up to volunteer on Saturday morning and do your bit for the community. It's booking the therapy appointment you keep avoiding. It's sending the email that actually reaches the person who can fix the thing. It's walking someone you love to the train station after a tough conversation. It's honouring your body's need to say no. It's small, boring, repeatable and it sure as hell moves things.

RUNNING IN THE 2025 FEDERAL ELECTION

As the 2025 federal election took shape, I made a decision that felt as terrifying as it was electric: I put my name forward to run as a candidate for the Australian Greens in the seat of Kingsford Smith. From the outside, it looked like the logical next step, the culmination of years spent taking meetings, drafting letters, fronting cameras, pushing the same message until it finally started to stick. I told myself I was taking everything I'd learned through advocacy – every survivor story I'd carried in my chest, every injustice I'd dragged into the light – and trying to carve it into law. I didn't want to just knock on doors, hoping someone would answer. I wanted a seat at the table where decisions are made, where policies are drafted, where futures are shaped. I wanted to bring voices that are usually erased into the heart of the system that erases them. I wanted a vote.

I told myself that was the reason. It wasn't the whole truth.

After I put my name forward, I felt that buzzing pride that surges when you step toward your boldest self. The boy who sat quietly in classrooms, the teenager who thought survival was the ceiling, was now preparing to ask an electorate to believe in him. It felt huge, but it felt right. And then something else moved in – not fear, not doubt, but something sharper: I wasn't just running because I wanted it. I was trying to prove something.

I've spent most of my life trying to earn the right to exist – turning pain into output, trying to make it 'worth it', sprinting ahead of shame and rage by becoming someone impossible to ignore. Someone my abusers couldn't ignore. The race quietly became a test I set for myself: if you can pull this off, maybe then you'll finally be enough. Enough for my father and stepmother to see they didn't get to write the ending. Enough for the little boy who never felt protected. Enough for the man who still scans rooms for his father's face. Enough for the invisible jury in my head, keeping score on whether I'd done 'enough' to deserve peace.

Even after years of therapy and advocacy, hypervigilance still hummed in my body. I moved through familiar streets like I was balancing on glass. The grocery store, the cafe, the park – places I knew how to survive in, but not how to relax in. For me, familiarity never meant safety so much as endurance. I confused surviving there with living there. I planned around the chance of seeing the people who had broken me and called that strength. It was routine, not freedom – a life inside a cage I'd learned to decorate.

Running from the same suburb where I was abused felt inevitable in a life built on vigilance. Of course you keep fighting. Of course you reclaim what was taken. Of course you sacrifice comfort, love and ease on the altar of control. Because if you stop, what are you worth?

That was the contract I'd signed with myself. Facing it almost broke me. But I asked the questions. What if healing isn't something you prove? What if it's something you allow? What if I am already enough – even if I never win a seat, never pass a law, never remake the system? What if joy doesn't have to be earned?

These questions changed everything. Running for parliament wasn't a betrayal of my healing, but it also wasn't the path to it. So – with hope intact and the purpose still there – I withdrew my submission to run for parliament and chose to be with the woman I love.

THE LOVE OF MY LIFE

For as long as I can remember, the idea of love, intimacy and relationships felt out of reach. My past experiences with trauma built that wall higher, and every attempt I made to cross it only reminded me of its strength. Love, vulnerability and the possibility of being exposed – fully known by another person – felt like they belonged to people without my scars and baggage. Navigating relationships after sexual trauma is complex, especially when those early experiences distort what love and connection look like. I told myself isolation was safer and intimacy was a luxury meant for other people.

Then I met Isabella Johnston.

It started the simple way: messages, long voice notes, FaceTimes until 4am. Bella slowly helped me unravel those beliefs of unworthiness. She brings a sense of adventure and fun to my life, turning ordinary moments into something I look forward to. Her boldness nudges me out of my comfort zone and wakes up parts of me I thought I'd lost. She's steady, a strength that completely anchors me. Her warmth softens my defences, makes it easier to let my guard down and be honest. She sees me for who I am and helps me treat myself with more compassion.

With Bella, connection feels possible. Day by day, it's like she holds up a mirror and says, 'Look at the real you. Look at the person beneath the scars.' She doesn't just say I'm worthy;

she helps me believe it – even when I forget, which happens often.

I think about the night we sat in a small restaurant in Ischia, Italy, where I took a leap of faith and had flown from Australia to meet her for the first time after months of talking online. The table between us was scattered with the remains of dinner, candles flickering low. Out of nowhere, she slid her hand across the table, took mine, looked me in the eyes, and said, 'What you went through was not your fault. I love you, and I accept every part of you – and that includes your daughter.'

The world went quiet. Her eyes didn't flinch. Her grip didn't loosen. Her words didn't stutter. There was no pity, no performance; just love. It was exactly what I needed to hear, even in the places I didn't have words for. The walls I'd built around my heart didn't collapse; they cracked, and let her in.

We tried to be sensible about what came after our three weeks in Italy together. She was heading to England for work. I had a life and responsibilities back in Australia. On paper, that should have been the end of it. But letting go felt wrong in a way I couldn't ignore. So we chose the harder thing: we tried long-distance.

And after six painfully long months in, the maths stopped working. The hours between us were chewing through the joy. I'd find myself staring at my calendar full of campaign meetings, community events, drafts for speeches and I'd then glance at the time in London and feel the split straight down the middle. I could keep telling myself that pushing harder was what made me worthy, that the next fight would finally quiet the old noise, or I could admit what had become obvious: I didn't want a life measured only in fights for justice. I wanted a life with Bella.

So I let myself say it out loud. I withdrew from the political run I'd started gearing up for, closed that chapter before it began, and chose to move to London to be with the love of my life. Because what Bella has given me isn't just love. It's peace. It's laughter in places I used to feel fear. It's excitement for what's new and what's still to come. It's the reminder that I am more than what happened to me, and that life can be gentle.

MOVING TO LONDON

Landing in London in March 2025 felt unreal, like stepping into a place I'd seen a thousand times but never thought I'd live in. Bright-red double-deckers whizzing past me, terraced houses with chipped paint and roses, a grey sky that could turn to light without warning. I'd get on the Tube and travel seven stops to work my retail job. After my shift, I'd stop at Sainsbury's and see the same security guard every day. Bella and I would cut through the park to the shops. I learned the smell of our stairwell, the sound our kettle makes before it clicks, the way the city hums at night. I started trying new things – new food, new routines, new ways of being. And somewhere in all of that, I kept thinking, *I live here. I can live simply.*

Then the quiet set in. No one expected me to prove my worth every morning by bleeding for it publicly, and after years of fighting, that felt completely abnormal. The silence pressed on my chest. I started thinking I was losing everything I'd built. If a law passed without me in the room, did I still count? If a meeting happened and I wasn't across the table asking the hard questions, was I still who I said I was?

I won't dress it up. I spiralled. Some days, the only sentence in my head was ugly and loud: *What's the point?* Some mornings, the thought of stepping in front of a bus on my way to work felt like relief.

What helped was saying it out loud – to the person I love, and to a doctor who listened – and then doing the ordinary things that keep you here. After five years off, I went back on antidepressant medication. I built a routine with boring things in it on purpose. I let my nervous system learn what life feels like without a siren of urgency in the background. I reminded myself that what felt boring was actually peace and safety.

There's a sentence I've said before and still believe: you cannot heal in the same environment that made you sick. London proved that, and then pushed me one step further. The environment mattered. Getting out of the streets in Sydney, stitched with old panic, mattered. Walking into stores where no one knew my story mattered. But it wasn't only the postcode that needed changing. The mindset – the part of me that measured worth by how much I could endure, that only felt useful when there was blood on the floor – had to change. Moving cities removed some triggers but it didn't remove the metric. I had to do that work myself – slowly, with a lot of back and forth. I had to stop using pain as proof.

Figuring out who I was outside of the fight was harder than I expected. My reflex, when something flares in the news, is still to stop everything I'm doing, draft a tweet, call a media contact and push for change. Sometimes I do, because it's needed. More often, now, I ask a different question first: will that actually help, or am I doing this because I'm afraid of being forgotten? A particular kind of guilt fades when you stop organising your entire identity around output. It doesn't vanish, and you don't undo years of conditioning in a few months, but there's relief in admitting the world's pain is not a daily test I must pass to be allowed peace. I can care, and I do, without making myself a hostage to every new outrage. I can be present with Bella without narrating the moment like a witness statement. I can hold the cause and also hold my life.

I still have days where I miss the version of me who could live on adrenaline and stay upright. Then I remember how much he was carrying and how often he looked over the edge. I don't treat rest like a moral failure.

London didn't fix me. It gave me space to let the fixing begin. It changed the backdrop so I could see what needed changing in the foreground. It gave me the chance to ask Bella to marry me – and she said yes! Most of all, it gave me room to build a life I don't want to escape from. That's the clearest sign this move was right, because I finally understood why I was doing it in the first place: so people like me could have a chance at exactly this. Two mugs drying by the sink. A toothbrush beside mine. Coats slung over the chair. Grocery bags on the bench. A future that isn't a performance. A life.

Not an exit from purpose, but a choice about how to carry it.

CHOOSING TO LIVE

After years of organising my days around the next fight, I can see now that the whole point of advocacy is never to live inside the fire forever. The point is to help build conditions where more of us could step out of it and live lives that feel safe, steady and ours.

I've done my bit. I've campaigned, started national conversations, initiated reviews which forced powerful people to look at what they'd rather leave alone. I've written this book, helped shift how people talk about character references for child sex offenders, and put words to things so the next survivor feels less alone – which might be the piece that matters to me most. There are still laws to pass and systems to fix and cultures to shift, and I know others will carry it next, as they always have, and I'll cheer them on and step in where I'm actually useful. But the metric I'm using now is different. It isn't how many doors I can kick open. It's whether I can sit at my own kitchen table and feel at peace. It's whether I can look in the mirror and not feel ashamed of what stares back at me. It's whether I can walk down the street with the woman I love and not scan every face for danger. It's whether I can be a dad in all the ordinary ways that matter. I now understand that my worth – and yours – cannot be held hostage to whether the machine says yes this week.

Advocacy had become a loop I couldn't get out of. It kept me in a constant state of trauma, urgency and conflict. My sense of self got swallowed. Most of my relationships revolved around conversations about harm and injustice. I was living in a cycle where my self-regard was tied to my ability to keep fighting the good fight. And in doing so, I forgot what it was like to just … live.

I've now worked out that, as an activist and survivor of childhood sexual abuse, the goal was never to stay in a place of re-traumatisation, constantly proving my value by showcasing how much I could endure. The point is to build a life that feels safe. Steady. Whole. Not one that is defined as purely 'happy' or 'sad', but one in which I am content. And right now, I am incredibly content.

I'm not disappearing. I'm not pretending the problems are solved. I'm just changing how I participate. These days, a lot of my advocacy happens in everyday moments: in conversations with colleagues at work, in catch-ups with friends at the pub, in the ways I call out harmful language or offer support when someone needs it. What I do now isn't smaller, it's just different. The public fights mattered, and they still do. But so does this kind of quiet, consistent advocacy that happens in real life, between people. Social media numbers and mentions in online articles might look impressive, but they're not the only measure of impact. Another metric is your ability to show up, person to person, and shift the way someone sees the world. It's the ripple effect you create in your immediate circles, the kind you can't chart with algorithms but that still changes lives. We all have the power to do that.

And I get that, in the world's current climate, this can sound like it comes from a place of privilege. But like so many people are realising, no one can carry a twenty-four-hour news cycle, global crises, personal battles and the endless push to change systems all at once without breaking. I don't want to reach the end of my life and realise I missed the moments right in front of me because I was too busy obsessing over whether a law passed, bracing for another meeting with a politician who doesn't give a fuck about people like me or spiralling over some stranger in my comments section insisting I was 'lucky' to be sexually abused by my stepmother. That is not living. That was my nervous system stuck on high alert, and me trying to convince myself it was purpose.

What matters to me now is not a list of headlines. It's a life. I want to be remembered as the father who loved his children more than anything, the husband who adored his wife for decades, the friend who left people lighter after they saw him, the son who cherished everything his mother did for him, the older brother who supported his siblings with kindness and the man who – despite enduring unimaginable pain – made the conscious choice to live. I want to reunite with my daughter and spend the rest of my life creating the ordinary, precious memories that were taken from us. I want to build a family with Bella that is gentle, grounded and full of love. A home where laughter is normal and safety is assumed, where we make our own rules and keep them simple: tell the truth, be gentle, rest when you're tired and ask for help.

If you've read this far, you already know how to make a difference. You've got the tools in your hands – how to start a petition, frame an argument, find allies, work with the media, pace yourself, build something that lasts. Use them when you need them. Start small and local. Or start big, if you must. Join something that's already moving. Hand the mic to someone who hasn't been heard yet. Push when pushing is needed, and then stop. Because stopping is not betrayal, it's what makes the work survivable. The goal was never to prove you can suffer endlessly for the greater good; the goal is to widen the circle of people who get to live a life they recognise as their own.

If you need permission to do the same, take it. You don't have to reopen your wounds to prove you've healed. You don't have to trade your peace for proof that you care. You don't have to earn the right to rest. You are allowed to step back without disappearing, to be proud without performing, to exist without explaining. Your worth isn't a scoreboard. It isn't the number of people you save, the meetings you sit through or the noise you can make online. It's the quiet way you move through the world. The softness in your voice, the steadiness in your love, the kindness you leave behind in rooms that will forget your name but not how you made them feel.

Purpose is not always a protest or a petition. Sometimes it's the call you answer, the friend you let stay over for the night, the way you choose gentleness when the world tells you to harden up. Change doesn't only happen within government. It happens in kitchens, in workplaces, in long silences where someone finally feels safe enough to tell the truth.

The law I've been fighting to change still hasn't passed as I write this. But that's not how I measure my worth anymore. Because my purpose was never just about a victory; it was about the courage to begin, and the refusal to let what hurt me become all that defines me.

I've spent years pouring everything I had into changing other people's lives. Now, I'm making sure I don't forget to live my own.

EPILOGUE

Since this book was written, Harrison James has changed the law.

On 3 December 2025, the Australian Capital Territory introduced legislation directly responding to the #YourReferenceAintRelevant campaign.

On 1 February 2026, the New South Wales Government went even further, introducing legislation to abolish the use of good character references in sentencing for all offences, extending well beyond the campaign's original aim.

Momentum for nationally consistent reform is now accelerating, and Harrison and his team continue to push for the complete abolition of good character references across Australia.

ACKNOWLEDGEMENTS

I always knew I wanted to write a book. I just didn't realise how agonising the task would be. The pain didn't come from the writing itself, but from what the writing pulled out of me. Despite the re-traumatisation, the resurfacing of old memories, the dark spirals of shame and the thoughts that dragged me back to places I never thought I'd return to, I know that I had to go through it all to get here. Every single page forced me to confront things I had buried. I needed to relive, rethink, and rewrite parts of my story that I once tried to forget. But I also know that without that process, I wouldn't have reached the reflective state of mind that closes this book in the final chapter. It's been cathartic in the truest, hardest sense of the word.

If I hadn't moved to London for love, if I hadn't paused public advocacy to focus on writing and if I hadn't pushed myself to my absolute breaking point this book simply wouldn't exist. And even if it somehow did, it wouldn't have the same heart. It's taken the right people, with the right insights and their overwhelming belief in me to help shape something so personal into something truly purposeful. For a first-time book, I could not be more proud of it. I hope it reaches those who need it most and helps them in their own journey of self-discovery. These are the people I want to thank for getting *Transform Your Pain Into Purpose* here.

Firstly, to the incredible team at Affirm Press: Kelly Doust, Laura Franks, Kevin O'Brien, Libby Turner and Kate O'Donnell. Thank you all for believing in me, and for giving this story a home. You saw the vision when it was still just a messy document written in airport lounges and share houses, and you treated it with care every step of the way.

Kelly, you specifically have been the heart of this process. You saw potential in me when all I could see was panic. You believed in this book, and in me, through every missed deadline and sleepless night. You balanced honesty with empathy and clarity with compassion. I couldn't have asked for a better publisher or a kinder human to walk alongside me in this.

This book wouldn't exist without the survivors who trusted me with their stories. You are the heartbeat of everything I do. Every message, every conversation, every moment of solidarity has shaped these pages more than you could ever know.

It also wouldn't exist without the people who've stood beside me since the beginning. My campaign co-founder and friend, Jarad Grice, who walked with me through every setback, breakthrough and long night of strategy. Grace Tame, whose courage showed me that truth, spoken clearly and without apology, can move mountains. Michael Bradley, who saw something worth pursuing in a young bloke with nothing but an idea and a gut feeling. Josh Byrnes and Alyssa James, whose bravery turned a campaign into a chorus.

To Bella, my partner and my peace. You held me through this while we were on the other side of the world away from our family and friends. Every dip in mood, every brainstorm, every challenge, you guided me with empathy, patience and love. So many of our back-and-forth conversations are baked into these pages. Thank you for being so generous with me, for holding space when I spiralled and for reminding me what matters. You've taught me that happiness can be safe, that softness is strength and that home can be a person. You're my soulmate, and I love you.

To my mum. Thank you for believing me from the very first moment I disclosed my abuse to you. You didn't question, you didn't hesitate, you just believed me. That moment changed everything, more than you'll ever know. It set me on a path toward healing. You've been my voice of reason when my thoughts go haywire, and you've reminded me, time and again, that I am not what happened to me. Your strength has carried me through the darkest of times that I didn't think I'd survive. You've lifted me up with your humour, and have made countless sacrifices throughout the years to make sure my own wellbeing came before yours. You had to take on the role of both a mother and a father, and there aren't enough words in the English language for me to express my gratitude for everything. I love you.

To my grandma, who gave me more than a roof over my head: you gave me a home full of warmth and love. I'll never forget the pride in your eyes when I started pursuing advocacy, or how you showed up to my first ever live speech like it was the grandest event in the world. You've celebrated every milestone like it was your own, and that enthusiasm has kept me going more times than I can count. You've loved me fiercely since the day I was born, and I hope I've made you proud.

And to my daughter, you were at the forefront of my mind when I wrote every word of this book. I'll never forget the day you were born: it was the first time in my life that I understood what unconditional love meant. I'll never forget the few memories we had together in those early years; I carry those moments with me like sacred treasures. There isn't a day that goes by that I don't think of you. I hope one day soon, we'll have the chance to know each other as we should have all along. I can't wait to give you the peace and love we both deserved from the very start. I cherish you beyond words, and I hope you grow up knowing just how deeply you are loved.

Thank you to the organisations who've walked this road beside me – Full Stop Australia, The Survivor Hub, Bravehearts, Polished Man, The Grace Tame Foundation, and SAMSN.

I am especially grateful to NSW Attorney General Michael Daley, NSW Premier Chris Minns and their teams; ACT Attorney General Tara Cheyne and Shane Rattenbury MLA; South Australian Attorney General Kyam Maher; Abigail Boyd MLC; Jaqui Scruby MP, and Michael Regan MP; and to federal parliamentarians including Zali Steggall MP, Senator Fatima Payman, Senator David Pocock, and Allegra Spender MP, whose willingness to listen and engage helped turn an idea into real reform. I also want to thank journalists and broadcasters including Shannon Molloy, Perry Duffin and Ray Hadley, and many others who gave this issue the attention it deserved.

None of this change happens alone. Reform is always the result of people who care enough to listen, and courageous enough to act.

And finally, to you, the reader – thank you for picking up this book, for sitting with the hard parts, and for daring to imagine something better. I could fill a hundred thousand pages trying to express my thanks to you. If these words have made you feel less alone, more seen, or even just a little braver, then it's all been worth it.

RESOURCES

If this book stirred within you a memory, a question, a feeling or a need for support, please know that you do not have to carry it alone. Healing doesn't happen in isolation, and there is real, compassionate help and community out there. These are some of the organisations and communities that have played a role in my own personal journey, or in the lives of countless others I've met along the way.

Full Stop Australia

Full Stop Australia offers 24/7 confidential counselling and information for anyone impacted by sexual, domestic or family violence. Their team are trauma-informed, deeply respectful, and genuinely care about the people they support. They also run the Survivor-Advocacy Ideas to Action Incubator Program, which is a powerful space where lived experience is turned into actionable, meaningful change. I've had the privilege of working alongside their team, and their integrity and warmth are second to none.

Their counsellors are available on 1800 FULL STOP (1800 385 578).

Website: www.fullstop.org.au

The Survivor Hub

The Survivor Hub is a community built by survivors, for survivors. It's a place to connect, rebuild, and heal through shared experience. Their MeetUps which I've personally attended and facilitated are grounding, safe spaces where you can share at your own pace, without pressure or judgment.

Website: www.thesurvivorhub.org.au

Survivors and Mates Support Network (SAMSN)

If you're a male survivor of child sexual abuse, SAMSN provides a supportive community of men who get it. Their groups are led by survivors and professionals, creating a space that's honest, validating and focused on recovery without shame. They also offer support for partners and family members of survivors.

Website: www.samsn.org.au

Bravehearts

Bravehearts has long been at the forefront of protecting children and supporting survivors of child sexual abuse in Australia.

They provide counselling, education and advocacy and continue to be a strong voice for prevention and reform.

Website: bravehearts.org.au

The National Office for Child Safety

The National Office for Child Safety is the Australian Government body dedicated to preventing child sexual abuse and strengthening child safety across all institutions and communities. Their work includes evidence-based research, national strategies, survivor-focused policy development and resources for parents, educators and organisations. Their site is a reliable starting point for understanding the scope of child sexual abuse in Australia and the frameworks designed to prevent it.

Website: www.childsafety.gov.au

If you need immediate support

If you or someone you know is in danger or needs crisis support, please reach out:

- 1800RESPECT (Australia): 1800 737 732 – 24/7 national counselling and support

- Lifeline: 13 11 14 – 24/7 crisis support and suicide prevention
- MensLine Australia: 1300 789 978 – counselling and support for men
- Kids Helpline: 1800 55 1800 – free and confidential counselling for children and young people

Recommended reading

Sometimes healing begins by hearing your story reflected in someone else's words, or by finally seeing the systems around you explained in a way that makes things click. These books and reports have shaped my own understanding of trauma, recovery, courage and the machinery that surrounds all of it, and I wanted to share with you for further reading and research.

Bite Back: Feminism, Media, Politics and Our Power to Change It All by Hannah Ferguson

A sharp, urgent exploration of how media and politics shape our understanding of gender, justice and power – and how we can reclaim our voices within it. Hannah's political insights have helped me better understand the systems I'm trying to change, and how to do that without losing heart in the process.

The Body Keeps the Score by Bessel van der Kolk

A groundbreaking look at how trauma reshapes both body and mind, and how we can reclaim our sense of safety through therapy, movement and connection.

The Ninth Life of a Diamond Miner by Grace Tame

Raw, unflinching and meticulously honest. Grace's memoir is one of the most powerful accounts of survival and truth-telling in this country.

The Gifts of Imperfection by Brené Brown

A gentle, grounding reminder that you don't have to be perfect to be worthy of love, belonging or a full life. Brené's definition of courage is so powerful that I actually quote it in Chapter 2 for this book. It's a beautiful companion for anyone learning to live with more self-compassion and less shame.

Daring Greatly by Brené Brown.

Another book from the phenomenal Brené Brown; this one is about the courage it takes to show up as your whole self, even when it feels risky or uncomfortable. It completely transformed how I think about vulnerability: not as weakness, but as one of the bravest things we can do. For me, it's a reminder that healing and connection both begin when we allow ourselves to be seen.

Final Report of the Royal Commission into Institutional Responses to Child Sexual Abuse – Identifying and Disclosing Child Sexual Abuse

(https://www.childabuseroyalcommission.gov.au/final-report)

One of the most comprehensive examinations of disclosure we've ever had. It explains why it takes survivors decades to speak, and why the system so often fails us.

A Brief Guide to the Royal Commission Final Report
https://www.childabuseroyalcommission.gov.au/sites/default/files/a_brief_guide_to_the_final_report.pdf

A more accessible entry point if the full report feels overwhelming. It breaks down the key findings and what they mean for real people.

NSW Recorded Crime Statistics – Quarterly Update (March 2024)
https://bocsar.nsw.gov.au/research-evaluations/2024/nsw-recorded-crime-statistics-quarterly-update-march-2024.html

This report provides the data behind what so many survivors already know: that only a fraction of sexual offences ever result in a conviction. It's a confronting but essential snapshot of reality in New South Wales.

Australian Bureau of Statistics – Childhood Abuse: Latest Release
https://www.abs.gov.au/statistics/people/crime-and-justice/childhood-abuse/latest-release

National data on childhood physical and sexual abuse, the relationships between victims and perpetrators, and patterns of disclosure. It gives context to how widespread this issue is across Australia, not just inside institutions.

Australian Child Maltreatment Study (2024)
https://www.acms.au/

A landmark national study examining the prevalence, nature, and impact of child abuse in Australia. It finds that one in three girls and one in five boys will experience child sexual abuse before they turn eighteen, equating to 28.5% of the population. Essential reading for understanding why survivor-led advocacy and systemic reform are so urgently needed.

REFERENCES

A Current Affair. (2024). Alyssa's parents wrote a character reference for her abuser. He avoided jail time. 9now.nine.com.au/a-current-affair/child-sex-abuse-survivor-character-reference-alyssa-james/99878bc3–1887–4302–885f-3f3bddec886e

Australian Associated Press. (2023, November 16). Sydney swim coach Paul Frost jailed for at least 24 years after grooming and sexually abusing 11 students. www.theguardian.com/australia-news/2023/nov/16/sydney-swim-coach-paul-douglas-frost-jailed-for-at-least-24-years-after-grooming-and-sexually-abusing-11-students

Australian Bureau of Statistics. (2023, November 22). Childhood abuse. https://www.abs.gov.au/statistics/people/crime-and-justice/childhood-abuse/latest-release

Australian Child Maltreatment Study. (2023, April 3). The prevalence and impact of child maltreatment in Australia: Findings from the Australian Child Maltreatment Study: 2023 Brief Report. www.acms.au/resources/the-prevalence-and-impact-of-child-maltreatment-in-australia-findings-from-the-australian-child-maltreatment-study-2023-brief-report/

Bromley, Harriet; Davis, Sarah K.; Morgan, Blaire; & Taylor-Dunn, Holly. (2023, May 18). The Professional Quality of Life of Domestic and Sexual Violence Advocates: A Systematic Review of Possible Risk and Protective Factors. pmc.ncbi.nlm.nih.gov/articles/PMC10913293

Brown, Brené. (2010, August 27). The Gifts of Imperfection: Let Go of Who You Think You're Supposed to Be and Embrace Who You Are. Hazelden Publishing.

Brown, Natalie. (2023, December 4). Victim-survivor Josh Byrnes joins Your Reference Ain't Relevant ACT campaign. Newscorp. www.news.com.au/lifestyle/real-life/news-life/victimsurvivor-josh-byrnes-joins-your-reference-aint-relevant-act-campaign/news-story/6785f429bfd01d123533ceadcb81b3b4

Brown, Natalie. (2024, July 31). Your Reference Ain't Relevant Campaign launches in South Australia. Newscorp. www.news.com.au/lifestyle/real-life/news-life/your-reference-aint-relevant-campaign-launches-in-south-australia/news-story/31bb13e432ef1f539f38e2e43b9d704c

Bureau of Crime Statistics and Research (BOCSAR). (2024, March). NSW Recorded Crime Statistics Quarterly Update: March 2024. https://bocsar.nsw.gov.au/documents/publications/rcs/rcs-quarterly/2024q1/NSW_Recorded_Crime_Mar_2024.pdf

Chung, Frank. (2024, July 31). Judges branded 'dumb smart people' as poll finds only 30 per cent of Australians have faith in court system. Newscorp. www.news.com.au/national/courts-law/judges-branded-dumb-smart-people-as-poll-finds-only-30-per-cent-of-australians-have-faith-in-court-system/news-story/de07eaca406c73b4c046617de99b7429

Danquah, Rudney; Lopez, Cristal; Wade, Laurel; & Castillo, Linda G. (2021, August 26). Racial Justice Activist Burnout of Women of Color in the United States: Practical Tools for Counselor Intervention. pmc.ncbi.nlm.nih.gov/articles/PMC8390016

Domestic Shelters. (2016, February 26). How Survivor Advocates Can Avoid Burnout: Secondary traumatic stress can affect those who help for a living. www.domesticshelters.org/articles/taking-care-of-you/how-survivor-advocates-can-avoid-burnout

Duffin, Perry. (2023, July 9). 'Punch in the guts': The law that is galling abuse survivors like Harrison. *The Sydney Morning Herald*. www.smh.com.au/national/nsw/punch-in-the-guts-the-law-that-is-galling-abuse-survivors-like-harrison-20230630-p5dktl.html

Grace Tame Foundation. (n.d.). The Harmony Campaign. www.thegracetamefoundation.org.au/projects-thc

Greens ACT. (2024, February 6). Petition to remove good character references for child sex abusers. greens.org.au/act/news/media-release/petition-remove-good-character-references-child-sex-abusers

James, Harrison. (2024, November 8). OPINION: Bonnie Blue's plan to sleep with 'barely legal' Schoolies is more than a headline-grabbing controversy. Mamamia. www.mamamia.com.au/bonnie-blue-schoolies/

Kraus, Krystalline. (2013, July 9). Activist Communique: Activists really know how to hurt each other. https://rabble.ca/politics/canadian-politics/activist-communique-activists-really-know-how-to-hurt-each

Legislation of New South Wales. (1999). Crimes (Sentencing Procedure) Act 1999, s 21A: 'Aggravating, mitigating and other factors in sentencing'. www5.austlii.edu.au/au/legis/nsw/consol_act/cpa1999278/s21a.html

Legislative Assembly for the Australian Capital Territory. (2023, October 23). Petition: Remove the Provision of Good Character References for Paedophiles in the Sentencing Procedure of Child Sexual Abuse Cases. epetitions.parliament.act.gov.au/details/e-pet-027–23

Longman, Molly. (2022, November 16). Activists Are Burning Out – No One's Picking Up The Pieces. Refinery29. www.refinery29.com/en-us/2022/11/11161927/non-profit-activist-work-unions-low-pay

Maiden, Samantha & Scanlan, Rebekah. (2024, November 16). Controversial sex worker Bonnie Blue's Australian visa cancelled over Schoolies stunt. Newscorp. www.news.com.au/lifestyle/real-life/news-life/controversial-sex-worker-bonnie-blues-australian-visa-cancelled-over-schoolies-stunt/news-story/5767cbf5fea8214efb168d3de6f6235a

Massola, James. (2024, July 30). We trust the police. But the court system? Not so much. *The Sydney Morning Herald/The Age*. www.smh.com.au/politics/federal/we-trust-the-police-but-the-court-system-not-so-much-20240723-p5jvu7.html

Molloy, Shannon. (2023, November 16). Famed Sydney restaurateur John Fink's "glowing" support for paedophile Paul Douglas Frost, who abused 11 children, sparks fury. Newscorp. www.news.com.au/lifestyle/real-life/news-life/famed-sydney-restaurateur-john-finks-glowing-support-for-paedophile-paul-douglas-frost-who-abused-11-children-sparks-fury/news-story/aa7ee3d9ef5fcbe6028b5b1ef9e060c7

National Office for Child Safety. (n.d.). How many people have experienced child sexual abuse? www.childsafety.gov.au/about-child-sexual-abuse/how-many-people-have-experienced-child-sexual-abuse

Parliament of New South Wales – Legislative Assembly. (2023, August

22). Petition: Remove good character references for paedophiles in the sentencing procedure of child sexual abuse cases. www.parliament.nsw.gov.au/lc/petitions/Pages/tabled-paper-details.aspx?pk=186308

Ratcliffe, Michelle. (2024, March 29). Social Workers, Burnout, and Self-Care: A Public Health Issue. pmc.ncbi.nlm.nih.gov/articles/PMC10987033

Rattenbury, Shane. (2024, May 8). Letter to Mr. Tom Duncan, Clerk of the ACT Legislative Assembly. epetitions.parliament.act.gov.au/details/e-pet-027–23/attachment/letter-from-the-attorney-general-government-response-to-petition-e-pet-027–23.pdf

Royal Commission into Institutional Responses to Child Sexual Abuse. (2017). Final Report – Volume 4: Identifying and Disclosing Child Sexual Abuse. www.childabuseroyalcommission.gov.au/sites/default/files/final_report_-_volume_4_identifying_and_disclosing_child_sexual_abuse.pdf

Sarigeorgiu, Elena. (2025, March 17). #Keep Girls on the Internet: Protecting Girls from Digital Gender-Based Violence. Girls Human Rights Hub. www.ghrh.org/blog/keep-girls-on-the-internet-protecting-girls-from-digital-gender-based-violence

Touma, Rafqua. (2024, May 29). Fewer than 10% of sexual assaults reported to NSW police end in a conviction, report finds. *The Guardian Australia*. www.theguardian.com/australia-news/article/2024/may/28/fewer-than-10-of-sexual-assaults-reported-to-nsw-police-end-up-proven-in-court-report-finds

Trauma Research UK. (n.d.). Healing through unsent letters. https://traumaresearchuk.org/healing-through-unsent-letters/

Twyford, Lottie. (2023, November 3). Mates Harrison James and Jarad Grice are on a mission to scrap good-character references for convicted paedophiles. ABC News. www.abc.net.au/news/2023–11–03/act-calls-remove-paedophile-sentencing-good-character-references/103057246